The Accademia Galleries in Venice

to my son Ezio

Translation
Ivor Neil Coward
Aaron Curtis
Nicolas Holland
Richard Sadleir

A better understanding and a fuller evaluation
of the works in the Accademia Galleries
have been made possible thanks in part
to the excellent restorations carried out by
the Soprintendenza speciale per il patrimonio
storico, artistico ed etnoantropologico
e per il polo museale della città di Venezia
e dei comuni della Gronda lagunare:
Rosa Bagarotto, Rossella Cavigli,
Luisa Gusmeroli, Chiara Maida,
Alfeo Michieletto, Luigi Sante Savio,
Gloria Tranquilli and Loretta Salvador.
Other contributions have been made by:
Egidio Arlango, Roberto Bergamaschi,
Erika Bianchini, Giulio Bono, Paola Borghese,
Lucia Castagna, Cooperativa C.B.C.,
Pierangela Formaggini, Stella Foscarini Volpin,
Anna Lisa Lusuardi, Corinna Mattiello,
Pierpaolo Monfardini, Thomas Charles Nelson,
Ottorino Nonfarmale, Sandra Pesso,
Marica Petkovic, Walter and Valentina Piovan,
Zelina Rado, Roberto Saccuman,
Claudia Vitturi, Ferruccio Volpin,
Marco and Serafino Volpin
and for recent scholarly research Ornella
Salvadori, Enrico Fiorin, Davide Bussolari
and the Istituto Nazionale di Ottica Applicata
(INOA)

Reprint 2017
First edition 2009

© Ministero dei Beni e delle Attività Culturali e del Turismo
Gallerie dell'Accademia di Venezia

An editorial production by
Mondadori Electa S.p.A., Milan

www.electa.it

Ministero dei Beni e delle Attività Culturali e del Turismo
Gallerie dell'Accademia di Venezia

The Accademia Galleries in Venice

Giovanna Nepi Scirè
with the collaboration of
Giulio Manieri Elia and Sandra Rossi

Selected bibliography compiled by
Debora Tosato

Electa

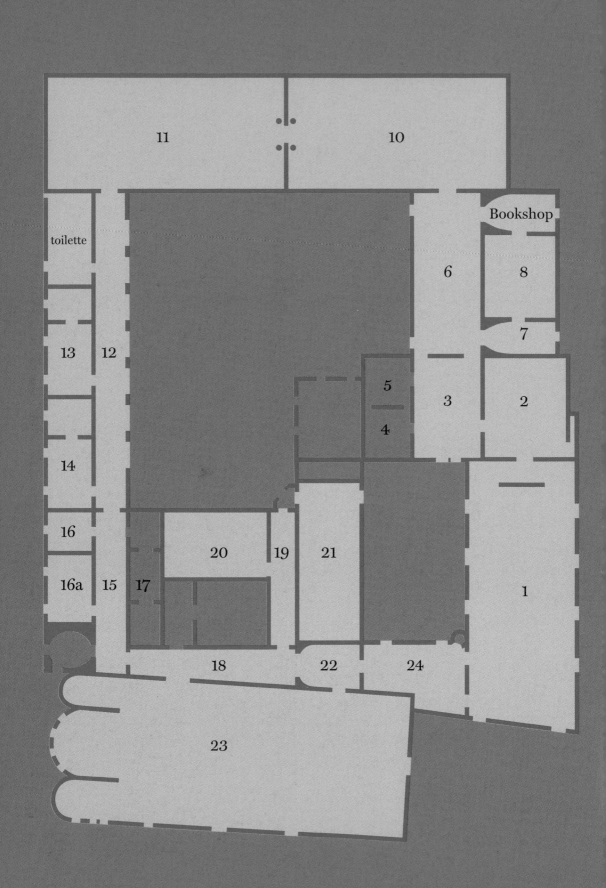

Contents

Introduction

Giovanna Nepi Scirè

In the early 1800s, the Accademia Galleries[1] along with the Brera Picture Gallery and Bologna Accademia became a museum. Its political origins were closely connected to the local events that in those years had reduced Venice to little more than a prize passed around among the great European powers.

With its annexation to the Kingdom of Italy under the Treaty of Pressburg on December 26, 1805, a series of decrees in 1806, 1808 and 1810 led to the closure of all the public buildings, forty parishes and 176 places of worship, while others were demolished. The works of art that surfaced from these events and which were somehow not sold or lost, found protection in the new Galleries.

Originally, however, the Galleries' purpose was largely educational, as is shown in the decree of September 10, 1803, extended on February 12, 1807, also to Venice, which established that—alongside an academy of fine arts divided into various faculties—there would be a gallery for the "benefit of those who practice painting."

The Venetian Academy of Fine Arts was forced to relocate from the Fonteghetto della Farina (flour warehouse) to a group of buildings—also acquired following the Napoleonic suppressions—which included the convent of the Lateran Canons, designed by Andrea Palladio in 1561, the Chiesa della Carità, reconstructed by Bartolomeo Bon

Canaletto
View of the church of Santa Maria della Carità, detail. National Gallery, London.

Giuseppe Borsato
Commemoration of Canova in the Scuola Grande della Carità.
Galleria Internazionale d'Arte Moderna, Ca' Pesaro, Venice.

between 1441 and 1452, and the Scuola della Carità, the first of the Venetian Scuole Grandi, founded in 1260. Thus there was also the problem of how to incorporate the works of art into structures whose original purpose was entirely different, and which were not connected to one another.

The Accademia faced problems from the start, due to its relative distance from the city center and its location on the other side of the Grand Canal before the bridge was built. This situation was described in a painting by Canaletto now on display in the National Gallery of London, which shows, among other things, the campanile that has since collapsed. A further problem was the limited amount of space available for use without resorting to a vastly expensive remodeling project for the Palladio building. Nonetheless, the government's decision was unshakable, and the Accademia—which had been considering the complex at Santi Giovanni e Paolo with its attached Scuola Grande di San Marco, or the Misericordia, or the church and monastery of Santa Caterina—found itself, instead, forcibly transferred to a location that was already recognized as completely inadequate.

The restructuring project was led by Giannantonio Selva and lasted until 1811. It was necessary to completely gut the church which, once the furnishings and altars were removed, was then divided horizontally and vertically to create five large rooms on the lower floor for the school and two on the upper floor to serve as exhibition rooms. These spaces were created after walling up the Gothic windows, with lighting coming from above. The buildings were connected by opening a passageway on the first floor at the back of the Sala dell'Albergo, and constructing a short stairway which led through a foyer to the other rooms.

The Scuola della Carità underwent minor renovations, important work having been carried out already during the eighteenth century under the direction of Giorgio Massari and Bernardino Maccaruzzi. In 1766 the ground floor entrance had been completely remodeled, while a few years earlier the façade had been renewed by opening the large doorway at the center; this made the old stairs obsolete, and they were demolished. In their place, two twin flights of stairs leading up to the Chapter Hall (Room 1) were constructed based on models by Maccaruzzi. The small façade remained which connected the church and school—and which served as the entrance to the school itself with the once colored statues depicting *Virgin and Child with Devotees*, commissioned from him by the Guardian Grande Marco Zulian (1345), and *Saint Christopher* and *Saint Leonard* (1378). The fourteenth-century doorway in the courtyard is still intact, although it has been walled in. It is topped by a colored stone lunette with the symbol of the Carità, commemorating the plague of 1348.

The rooms of the Scuola della Carità were largely left unaltered: the wooden ceiling from the late fifteenth century is still in the Sala dell'Albergo (Room 24), as is the triptych by Antonio Vivarini and Giovanni d'Alemagna dated at 1446, and Titian's *Presentation of Mary at the Temple* which dates from August 1534 to March 1539. The other canvases in the cycle—the *Marriage of the Virgin* by Giampietro Silvio and the *Annunciation* by Girolamo Dente, formerly in the Parish of Mason Vicentino, are now in the museum's storerooms.

Also intact—aside from the fact that the altar was removed—is the great Chapter Hall (Room 1), where the sumptuous ceiling remains on display with its deep blue and gold lacunars, carved by Marco Cozzi from 1461 to

1484. Originally there were five high reliefs depicting the *Madonna della Misericordia* and the symbols of the other Scuole Grandi. They were removed in 1814 and disappeared thereafter, replaced today by the *Holy Father* at the center which has been attributed to Pier Maria Pennacchi and was originally in the Venetian oratory of San Girolamo, and by the four *Prophets* by Domenico Campagnola also attributed to Stefano dell'Arzere, from the Scuola della Madonna del Parto in Padua.

It proved decidedly more difficult to adapt the Palladian convent, however, especially since its integrity had already been somewhat compromised by a fire in 1630. To provide greater exhibition surface Selva approached it with caution: the arcades of the Ionic loggia were closed leaving some half-moons for lighting; the windows on the Sant'Agnese canal were raised, and the cells on the top floor were modified to create the engraving school and lodgings for the professors.

Beginning on August 10, 1817, the Gallery was opened to the public for a brief period, and had a great number of visitors. A painting made by Giuseppe Borsato in 1822 commemorating Canova portrays with almost photographic precision how the first room must have looked at the Accademia's opening—with not only the Veneto paintings of the sixteenth century, but also Titian's *Assumption* from the Frari, which had been secured in 1816 by the president Leopoldo Cicognara.

The first items to be included in the collection were: a small number of works being, donations and trial works by the academicians which were brought over from the old Academy; some of the remaining paintings from the Scuola della Carità; Abbot Farsetti's collection of plasters, acquired from the Austrian government in 1805. Pietro Edwards, who was named the curator of the collection,

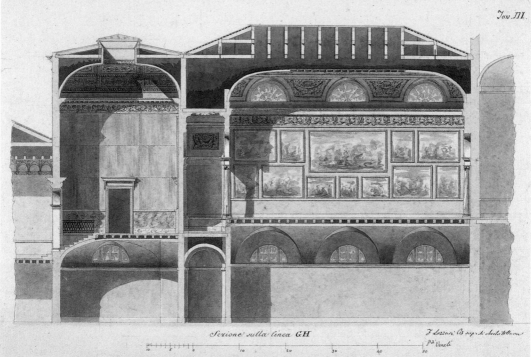

Francesco Lazzari
*Section of the tribunes with the project
for the installation of Titian's "Assumption"
and Canova's "Theseus Slaying a Centaur."*
Correr Museum, Drawings and Prints Room, Venice.

Francesco Lazzari
*Section of the room used as a picture gallery
and of the ground floor rooms.* Correr Museum,
Drawings and Prints Room, Venice.

had been in charge of public paintings from 1778 until the fall of the Republic. All the governments that followed in Venice found in him a highly competent and useful collaborator. He was employed by the French commissaries for the selection of the pieces to be given to Napoleon in 1797, and performed a similar function under the Austrians and the Kingdom of Italy, at which time he received the title of "curator of state-owned holdings." However, the overlapping of responsibilities—at times contradictory—with the Accademia Galleries placed him in an ambiguous situation, and did not allow him to block the mass exodus of important pieces to Milan or the dispersion of many important works. Although the next secretary of the Accademia, Antonio Diedo, was responsible for choosing state-owned works destined for the Gallery itself, during the prolonged delivery period the more important works went to the Brera Gallery in Milan, while Titian's *Saint John the Baptist* was kept in Venice (from the church of Santa Maria Maggiore) only because of the mass outcry of the Venetian people. Luckily some paintings were added that France had returned, among which was Paolo Veronese's famous *Feast in the House of Levi*. Others were removed from Venetian churches, such as that of San Giobbe, and placed in the Accademia Galleries as a precautionary measure, and yet other paintings were added from the first private contributions to the Gallery.

Important works were added to the Gallery by bequest: in 1816 Girolamo Molin provided many works including an interesting group by early painters that contained the *Stories from the Passion* attributed to Giovanni Baronzio, triptychs by Alberegno and Jacobello del Fiore, the polyptych by Lorenzo Veneziano with the *Annunciation* and Giambono's *Paradise*. Canova's brother then donated the

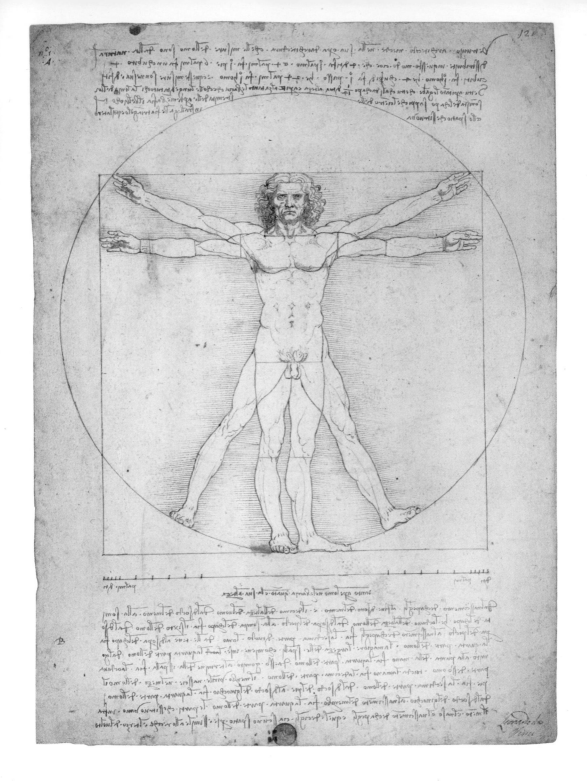

Leonardo da Vinci
Vitruvian Man.

large plasters *Theseus Slaying a Centaur* and *Hercules and Lica*, now on deposit at the Gipsoteca (Plaster Gallery) of Possagno. In 1833 (finalized in 1850) the bequest of Felicita Renier was added, with works such as *Saint Jerome* by Piero della Francesca, the *Madonna and Child with Saints Paul and George* and the *Virgin and Child with Saints Catherine and Magdalene* by Giovanni Bellini, and Cima's *Pietà*. Lastly, in 1838 Girolamo Contarini donated his noteworthy collection of 188 paintings, which included Bellini's *Madonna degli Alberetti*, the *Virgin with Standing Blessing Child* and the *Allegories*, Cima's *Madonna and Child between Saints John the Baptist and Paul*, the *Mystic Marriage of Saint Catherine* by Boccaccio Boccaccino, the *Sacred Conversation* attributed to Sebastiano del Piombo and six Venetian scenes by Pietro Longhi.

Some acquisitions—which were significant although relatively few considering the enormous availability on the market—further enriched the heritage. The collection nevertheless continued to favor and protect Venetian painting, as it does now, and so was not particularly suitable for a well-rounded artistic education. During the 1800s, much effort was made to balance out this situation until the end of the century, when interest in the educational aspect had all but vanished and with it the desire to expand the breadth of the Gallery's collection.

Nonetheless, in 1822 the Accademia anticipated the intentions of the Brera Gallery and, through Abbot Celotti, acquired Giuseppe Bossi's prestigious drawing collection, which boasted more than 3,000 pieces and included—in addition to folios by Leonardo da Vinci among which the famous *Vitruvian Man*—several preparatory sheets for the *Battle of Anghiari*, drawings by Michelangelo, Raphael, Perugino, Giovanni Bellini, the Bolognese, Roman, Tuscan, Ligurian and Lombard Schools, as well

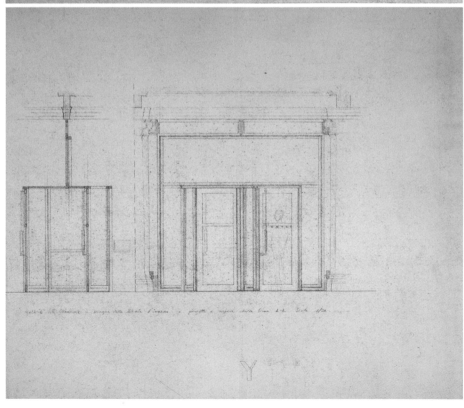

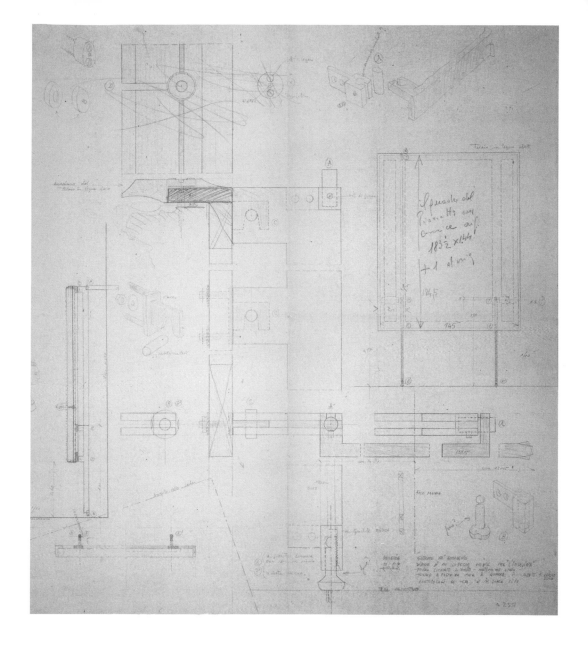

Carlo Scarpa
Project for the awning
for the *Madonna*
by Paolo Veneziano, Room 1.

Carlo Scarpa
Project for the compass
in the entrance.

Carlo Scarpa
Project for the support
for Giambattista Piazzetta's,
The Fortune Teller, Room 16a.

as German, French and Flemish Schools. Two years later, again through Celotti, a body of 602 drawings from Giacomo Quarenghi was secured.

As the number of artworks increased, the exhibition spaces became wholly insufficient and overcrowded. The plans for enlargement designed by Selva, who died in 1819, were carried out under the supervision of Francesco Lazzari, and provided for two large halls to the left of the Palladian convent (Rooms 10 and 11). In 1828 both these halls were built, and the first one was opened; the second was not completed until 1834. Between the two halls four Greek marble columns were transferred from the Scuola della Misericordia. In 1829 Lazzari completely remodeled the convent: in the courtyard he demolished the arches inspired by Palladian perspective and left intact by Selva, and expanded the ends with two intercolumniations. He reopened the walled up Ionic arches, which at a later date, along with the Doric arches, were fitted with large windows.

In 1830 the façade was also modified: the emblems of La Carità were replaced with those of the Accademia, windows were opened in the niches, and a sculpture—now in the Public Gardens—by Antonio Giacarelli of *Minerva Seated upon the Adriatic Lion* was placed at the top.

During this time, the large room on the ground floor was divided, giving the Galleries a separate entrance from that of the Scuola (shown also in Combatti's plan of 1847). It was also in this period that the painters and students of the Accademia decorated the lunettes on the ceiling of the first room with portraits of the most important Veneto artists, replacing previous works that are now indecipherable. Lastly, between 1849 and 1856, all the rooms were connected together, with the construction of the *sale nuovissime* ("newest rooms," nowadays Rooms 6, 7, 8 and 9).

The collections were further expanded at this time, above all by the purchase from Emperor Franz Joseph in 1856 of several important paintings in the Manfrin Gallery, such as the *Madonna* by Nicolò di Pietro, *Saint George* by Mantegna, Memling's *Portrait of a Young Man*, Giovanni Agostino da Lodi's *Washing of the Feet* and *The Old Woman* by Giorgione.

Initially, the annexation to the Kingdom of Italy did not bring about large-scale changes but, from 1870 onwards, the school gradually became separate from the Accademia Galleries. This took place through various stages, including decrees in 1878 and 1879. The collection, entrusted to the supervision of the president of the Accademia, was officially delivered to him on January 15, 1881, while on March 13, 1882, final independence was sanctioned for both the school and the Accademia Galleries.

In 1895 the director, Giulio Cantalamessa, oversaw a radical reorganization of the painting collection, including a new home for the *Assumption* (Room 2) based on a project by Giacomo Franco of 1886. By eliminating works by artists of the 1800s and consolidating the few paintings from other Italian and foreign schools, he tried for the first time to establish a chronological order. The unitary cycles from the fifteenth-century schools of San Giovanni Evangelista and Sant'Orsola—formerly dispersed—were regrouped into two rooms of the church. The *Legend of Saint Ursula* cycle was housed in one of the new octagonal spaces, with lighting from above, that would not actually replicate their original space (also due to insufficient information in that regard), but rather would serve to enhance the continuity of the pictorial narrative. Sixteenth-century Veneto paintings were placed in the large halls. Reacting probably to public opinion, Cantalamessa

returned Titian's *Presentation of the Mary at the Temple* to the Sala dell'Albergo, where it had been located until 1828, believing correctly that it was preferable to respect the vision of the artist regarding the positioning and scanty lighting of the painting. The eighteenth-century stone benches were then replaced with the sixteenth-century dossals seen today. He also removed the bronzes (the plasters were already on deposit at the Scuola where they were used for educational purposes), which were later brought together again in the Franchetti Gallery at Ca' d'Oro. Cantalamessa thus established what has remained the primary focus of the Accademia: a collection of Veneto painting from the fourteenth to the eighteenth century. Cantalamessa also enriched the collection, adding *Saints*

Accademia Galleries, church of the Carità, view with the canvases of the Sala dell'Albergo of the Scuola di San Marco.

Peter and Paul by Crivelli, the *Madonna and Child* by Cosmè Tura, Basaiti's *Saint George*, Palma il Vecchio's *Sacred Conversation*, the *Mystic Marriage of Saint Catherine* by Lorenzo Veneziano, Paolo Veronese's *Hercules and Ceres*, and two early works by Tiepolo. Cantalamessa was succeeded by Gino Fogolari in 1905, and little was done to the Accademia itself, although the collection of drawings and paintings continued to expand under his long direction, with the acquisition of two more early works by Tiepolo, various pendants, the *Death of the Virgin* by Pennacchi, the organ doors by Bellini originally at the Miracoli, Romanino's *Lamentation over the Dead Christ*, the *Crucifixion of Saint Peter* by Luca Giordano, Strozzi's *Supper*, the *Portrait* by Fra' Galgario, Paolo

23

Veneziano's *Madonna*, Tiepolo's draft of *The Exaltation of the Cross*, and lastly in 1932 Giorgione's *Tempest*. After World War I, Fogolari lobbied for important pieces of art which had originally belonged to Venice to be returned from Austria.

During the war, the most important paintings had been kept in Florence. From 1921 to 1923, as these pieces were being returned, the museum was again remodeled.

The Accademia suffered the loss of Titian's *Assumption*, which was returned to the church of the Frari; the room that had been designed for the large canvas seemed and remains disproportionate. The two rooms dedicated to the canvases of the *Ursula* cycle and the *Cross* cycle were eliminated, creating one large space with apses and restoring the truss ceiling and the Gothic windows on the side walls. The canvases with the *Miracles of the Cross* remained there, while the *Stories of Saint Ursula* were displayed in the small room where they are still kept today (Room 21): a largely arbitrary reconstruction of the room with choir stalls and backs from other locations.

A more "original" arrangement was given to the rooms dedicated to the small eighteenth-century works (Room 17), incorporating imitation materials and an antique door originally from the Ca' Rezzonico. Eighteenth-century doors, probably from a palazzo in Brescia and painted by Pietro Scalvini and Saverio Gandini were purchased in 1912 and installed in the Palladian loggia, where they are still seen today. As under the direction of Cantalamessa, once again the works from the nineteenth century were removed and placed in storage at Ca' Pesaro; a similar fate awaited the paintings from foreign schools, which were moved to the Franchetti Gallery at Ca' d'Oro. The immediate need to implement more modern criteria for the museum reached its culmination during the 1940s, and especially after direction of the Accademia passed to Vittorio Moschini in 1941. Moschini worked with Carlo Scarpa even while World War II was underway to formulate a more articulate restructuring, including the construction of a large new building to be added to the nineteenth-century halls. The urgency to rebuild other Italian museums made it impossible to carry out the vast transformations that they had planned, but nonetheless a renovation project was begun which marked the end of a museum model that had remained unchanged since the turn of the century.

Work was begun in 1945 and lasted until 1960, involving the drastic elimination of the older rooms, carpeting, wooden skirting boards, imitation frames; these materials were replaced with a more neutral plaster with a special grain, warm-toned woods, jute, fustian, iron and glass, all carefully chosen and meticulously arranged. Given the space limitations and the fixed position of some of the larger canvases, a more logical itinerary through the museum was sought out, with a more careful selection of the works on display. The following year, the *Miracles of the Cross* paintings were regrouped in a special room built in 1949 (Room 20) next to the hallway leading to the "Ursula" Room, and the two rooms—which were to house the closely related cycles—were connected by a small platform. As a result of this first project, which was improved later in 1959 and 1960, the room assumed its present appearance. Also in 1947, the furnishing and arrangement of the "Ursula" Room was completed, eliminating the previous design—which was completely anachronistic—and also that of the eighteenth-century rooms, combining them into one larger room.

The following year, extensive imitation parts of the original wall decoration were removed from the church, and four new skylights were added to provide light from above. The fifteenth-century paintings were arranged on panels, almost giving the appearance of a temporary exhibition, out of respect for the original architectural structure. Between 1950 and 1952 the first room was reorganized: the windows which had been walled in during the nineteenth century to increase the display area were re-opened, and some fragments of late fourteenth-century frescoes were revealed along the walls, while the view into the disproportionate room (originally for Titian's *Assumption*) was blocked with a wide brick panel where the *Lion Polyptych* by Lorenzo Veneziano was to be placed. Between 1950 and 1953 the new entrance was created with its now famous compass, while in 1955 Rooms 4 and 5 were completed for the display of small-sized masterpieces and Giorgione's *Tempest*, finally removed from the isolated pre-war location.

Under the direction of Francesco Valcanover from 1961 to 1977, special attention was given to the improvement of services, from the most basic ones to the installation of new fire prevention and anti-theft systems. Further efforts were dedicated to the preservation of drawings, collected on the top floor in air-conditioned rooms and special cases. The museum was equipped with more rational and efficient storage facilities, while in the church in the room opposite the apses a space was created dedicated to Gino Fogolari for temporary exhibitions and shows. The collection did not grow in the years immediately after the war.

In 1949 Guido Cagnola generously donated a notebook of sketches by Canaletto depicting various Venetian scenes, an invaluable document for tracing the creative process in his paintings. Acquisitions were made again in the 1970s:

in 1971 *Fire at San Marcuola* by Francesco Guardi w
added, as was Mantegna's panel with *Saint Peter and
Devotee*; in 1979 Count Nani Mocenigo sold the larg
Longhi painting of *The Family of Procurator of St. Mark's
Luigi Pisani*; in 1981 the *Portrait of the Knight Giovanni
Grimani* by Strozzi was obtained from Palazzo Barbaro
Curtis through a purchase option; in 1982 the *Stories of
Doge Tommaso Mocenigo* by Filippo Zaniberti and Mat-
teo Ponzone, formerly in the Palazzo Mocenigo; in 1983
Jacopo Bassano's *Adoration of the Shepherds* was acquired
from the Giusti del Giardino family. In 1987 two *Putti
with Plaques* and two allegories of Justice and Patience
were obtained, remnants of the ceiling made by Giorgio
Vasari in 1542 for a room in Palazzo Corner on the Grand
Canal. In 2002 a third *Putto with a Plaque* was recovered
and the Gallery obtained the deposit of the central part
depicting *Charity* from the Brera in Milan, where it was
in storage. At the same time the negotiations were undertaken for the acquisition of the two surviving panels of
Faith and *Religion*, both in private collections in London.
Unfortunately the negotiations came to nothing.
In 1983, after the death of Rodolfo Siviero—the former
head of the office for the recovery works of art "exported"
to Germany before and during World War II, and to other
countries in later years—Francesco Valcanover successful-
ly and courageously recovered at least thirty works from
those that had been returned from abroad, and which
had remained in Palazzo Pitti in Florence for decades
while delivery plans were stalled and delayed.
Unfortunately the returned works were always fewer than
those requested, but in 1988 seven paintings were
obtained, including an episode from *Jerusalem Delivered*
by Giannantonio Guardi, an artist who was not previously present in the Galleries, two small *Bacchanalia* by

ebastiano Ricci, and two *Capricci* attributed to Canaletto and his workshop.

In 1989 *Paesaggio con frati in preghiera (The Great Wood)* by Anton Francesco Peruzzini and Alessandro Magnasco was acquired through a purchase option. In 1995 Giuseppe Angeli's *The Tickle* was acquired, and in 1997 thirteen large drawings by G.B. Piazzetta, formerly in the Alverà collection, were obtained.

In 2003 a drawing by Gaetano Previati depicting a female nude was acquired by compulsory purchase as it was about to be exported to France. In 2006 a bequest by Bianca De Feo Leonardi brought the sketch for the ceiling of the church of the Gesuati by Giambattista Tiepolo. The acquisitions in 2006 also included a copper plate with *Studies of Hands* by Antonio Zecchin, after a drawing by Francesco Bartolozzi, and Francesco Salviati's *Offering to Psyche Worshipped as Venus*, which comes from the ceiling of Palazzo Grimani. The following year the fine *Portrait of a Lady* by Girolamo Forabosco enriched the seventeenth-century collection, a bequest from Guido Zattera. Finally, the right of purchase was exercised for the *Study of a Male Nude* by Pompeo Batoni, when it was presented to the export office for transfer to London.

In 1988, after the exhibition of the restoration of works by Paolo Veronese, his painted ceilings were concentrated in Room 6. In 1995 the Gallery was opened in the long wing on the second floor of the Palladian cloister. It was used to display some eighty masterpieces formerly kept in storage. In 1996 the display in Room 11 was redesigned to present all the surviving fragments by Giambattista Tiepolo from the destroyed ceiling of the church of the Scalzi. Subsequently the display in the church of the Carità was completed with canvases formerly in the Sala dell'Albergo of the Scuola di San Marco. Finally, optical fiber lighting was installed in Rooms 4 and 5 and in the small gallery of eighteenth-century masterpieces.

In 1997 a sales point was added in Room 9, while two windows were reopened in Room 6 to give a view of the Palladian façade.

In 2005, after the Academy of Fine Arts moved to the complex of the Ospedale degli Incurabili (restored at the expense of the Ministry for Cultural Heritage and Activities), extensive work began to double the exhibition spaces, remove architectural barriers and provide the museum with all the facilities and services today indispensable to the functioning of such an institution: the wardrobe, rest and recreational spaces, including amenities for the disabled, exhibition and conference rooms with an independent entrance, sales points and a cafeteria accessible also from the outside, etc.

The alterations will also provide free access to the Palladian courtyard, previously closed to the public.

In the last two years alterations have been made to the installation to ensure the best safety conditions, with a commitment to carrying out the work while keeping the museum open to the public.

This volume presents the state of the display in 2009, when the work is still in progress: for this reason it does not include many of the works of the seventeenth century and nineteenth century which, though of outstanding quality and widely represented in the Gallery's holdings, will be on display only when the new spaces are completed with the extensions to the museum.

[1] The present introduction draws particularly on S. Moschini Marconi, *Gallerie dell'Accademia di Venezia. Opere d'arte dei secoli XIV e XV*, Rome 1955; see also: E. Bassi, *Il complesso palladiano della Carità*, Milan 1980 and G. Nepi Scirè, *I capolavori dell'arte veneziana. Le Gallerie dell'Accademia di Venezia*, Venice 1991. For the history of the Gallery's collection of graphic works see also G. Nepi Scirè, *Storia della collezione dei disegni*, Milan 1982.

1 The "Primitives"

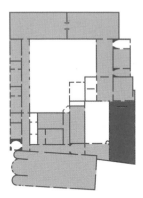

This was the room where the Chapter met of the Scuola di Santa Maria della Carità, one of the six Scuole Grandi of Venice. These schools were powerful secular guilds for devotion and assistance to the poor. The ceiling, which was built between 1461 and 1484 by Marco Cozzi of Vicenza—at the time a member of the Scuola—is made up of square lacunars with leaf decorations on the side and heads of angels with eight wings, each with different facial characteristics. The blue background and the original colors of the figures have resurfaced from under the gilt decoration made in the 1700s thanks to a long restoration project completed in 1992. The paintings in the compartments, however, do not belong to the original decoration: at the center is the *Holy Father*, probably the work of Pier Maria Pennacchi (1464–1514/15), while at the corners are the four Prophets attributed to Domenico Campagnola (1500–1564) or Stefano dell'Arzere (recorded from 1540 to 1575).

The polychrome marble floor dates to the remodeling of the 1700s. The rooms underwent other modifications at the beginning of the 1800s, when the entire complex of buildings became the Accademia: the back altar was removed, the windows were walled over to increase exhibition space and the original paintings were replaced with works that were to form the new gallery (including Titian's *Assumption*, later returned to the church of the Frari). The present-day configuration of the room is the work of Carlo Scarpa, begun in 1950. Scarpa reopened the windows, restored the fragments of the late fourteenth-century fresco along the walls and arranged the gold backed paintings on the wooden panels with the iron bases that still support them today. Over the course of 2004 all the works in the room have been subjected to special maintenance; Scarpa's panels have been restored. In the course of 2007 the famous display case containing the Cross of Saint Theodore was also restored.

**Master of Ceneda
(Ercole del Fiore?)**
*Coronation of the Virgin
in Paradise with Donor*, detail.

1

Jacobello del Fiore
(recorded in Venice
from 1401 to 1439)
1. *Justice Enthroned between
the Archangels Michael
and Gabriel*
(*Triptych of Justice*)
Panels with gilded plaster
decorations, 208 × 194 cm
(central panel), 208 × 133 cm
(Saint Michael), 208 × 163 cm
(Saint Gabriel)
Cat. 15
Acquisition: 1884,
following the suppressions
Latest restoration: 2006–07

Painted in 1421 for the seat
of the Magistrato del Proprio
at the Doge's Palace, which
oversaw the civil and penal
court. In the central panel
between two lions—symbols
of divine wisdom (alluding
to the throne of Solomon)—
is Justice, who holds
a sword in the right hand
and scales in the left.
The closest iconographic
source for Saint Michael,
who holds up the scale
while slaying the dragon,
is found in a mosaic
in St. Mark's baptistery.
On the Latin writings
between the scrolls, the
archangel Gabriel entreats
the Virgin to guide men in
the darkness of their actions,
while Michael, the warrior
angel and defender of the
Church—in his dual role
as judge of souls and fighter
against the dragon, a symbol
of Satan—asks her to levy
rewards or punishments
according to merit.
The wording behind Justice
"I will carry out the wishes
of the angels and the holy

words, be mild towards
the pious, enemy of the evil
and disdainful of the proud"
is generally attributed
in Nordic art to Christ
the Judge.
Justice is clearly identified
with Venice, as it is also
represented in the relief on
the west façade of the Doge's
Palace. The Venice-Justice
symbolic association, and
that of Peace is here enriched

by the Virgin Mary, since
peace and justice were
fundamental ideological
concepts of the Venetian
State.
An important official
commission, with complex
symbolism, the triptych
shows the influence
of Gentile da Fabriano and
fully embodies the courtly
Gothic spirit. It was to be
an important model above

all for Michele Giambono
and Michele di Matteo.
On the far right, the frame,
with the original gilding
and coloring, has the arms
of Tommaso Mocenigo,
doge from 1414 to 1423.

2

Paolo Veneziano
(active from 1333 to 1358;
died before 1362)
2. *Coronation of the Virgin Polyptych*
Panels, gold ground,
98 × 63 cm (central),
94 × 40 cm each (four sides),
26 × 19 cm (above six larger panels), 23 × 7 cm (above four smaller panels),
30 × 16 cm (the two top panels)
Cat. 21
Acquisition: 1812, following the suppressions. The central panel, which was taken to Brera by mistake in 1908, was united with the complex only in 1950
Latest restoration: 1951

At the center, the Coronation of the Virgin. At the sides, the Stories of Christ. On the upper part, at left: the Pentecost, Saint Matthew, the Vestment of Saint Claire, Saint John, Saint Francis Gives His Clothes to His Father; at right, Saint Francis Receiving the Stigmata, Saint Mark, the Death of Saint Francis, Saint Luke, Christ the Judge. At the center: the two prophets Isaiah and Daniel.
The polyptych comes from the church of Santa Chiara, as is attested by the Franciscan images in the upper part, and especially—in the Death of Saint Francis episode—the presence of the small monk, probably the commissioner of the work. Dating to around 1350, it documents the insertion of mainland motifs into the Byzantine influenced culture of Venice, also revealed in the *Coronation of the Virgin* of 1324 in the National Gallery of Washington. These motifs become more complex here, with decorative effects and more accentuated Byzantine traits; indeed, the Byzantine influence in Paolo's work has led some to suggest that he traveled to Constantinople, where he obtained the new elements he would later introduce in his paintings. The piece reveals great diversity between the small side episodes and the larger central figures, which are extraordinarily refined arabesques.
This divergence does not, however, allow us to suggest that other hands were involved in the creation of the composition, especially given the consistently high quality of the work.
The artist alternates the courtly and precious Byzantine language of the central part, with its fixed iconic nature that well suits the depiction of an event taking place outside normal time and space, with precise references to the Western cultural affinity for the narrative unfolding of "stories."

3

Paolo Veneziano
(active from 1333 to 1358;
died before 1362)
3. *Virgin and Child Enthroned with Two Donors*
Panel, gold ground,
142 × 90 cm, 157 × 105 cm with the original frame
Cat. 786
Acquisition: 1913, from the Salvadori antiquary of Venice
Latest restoration: 1952

The piece was acquired in 1913. While the original two-tone "toothed" frame and the old crossed support on the back are still intact, the work has lost the veiling of the flesh-tones, the lower inscription and some of the colors in the dress of the Virgin. It was first recognized as a work of Paolo Veneziano in the catalogue of 1928, and today it is unquestionably accepted as such.
Its similarity to the 1321 *paliotto* at Dignano, which the painting slightly postdates, points to its having been produced in the second half of the 1330s.
The Virgin with the Infant Jesus in the clypeus constitutes a Syrian iconographic variant of the Platytera, while the gesture of sheltering the two small devotees, whose physical details make them veritable portraits, is an unusual reminder of the *Madonna della Misericordia*. The monumentality of the image of the Virgin—"dark-faced like a Coptic or Cretan inspired icon"—and the harmonious assimilation of Eastern and Western elements, together with the humanity of the commissioners, make this arguably the artist's masterpiece.

Room 1

4

colors and the elegance of its figures which show the influence of Gentile da Fabriano. It was completed after 1427, when there was still a wooden crucifix on the altar. It is likely that the commissioner was probably Galeazzo Borromeo, nephew of Alessandro, who had the chapel restructured to place his tomb here.

Lorenzo Veneziano
(recorded in Venice from 1356 to 1372)
5. *Saint Peter* and *Saint Mark*
Panel, gold ground, 115 × 42 cm, 115 × 64 cm
Cats. 5, 5a
Acquisition: 1812, following the suppressions
Latest restoration: 1948

Signed and dated 1371, these are the side panels of a disassembled polyptych. The center panel (the *Resurrection*) is kept at the Museo Civico of Milan. The association of the founder of the Church with the protector of the Venetian state and the fact that the work comes from the Silk Office at Rialto reveal the diffusion of religious devotion in the public life of the city.

Giovanni da Bologna
(recorded from 1377 to 1389)
6. *Madonna of Humility, Annunciation, Saints John the Baptist, John the Evangelist, Peter, Paul and Members of the Scuola di San Giovanni Evangelista*
Panel, gold ground, 111 × 99 cm
Cat. 17
Acquisition: 1812, the following the suppressions
Latest restoration: 1948

A work from the early 1380s. Connections between the artistic culture of the Venetian lagoon and that of the Emilia region are evident here, for example in the naturalism of the flowery meadow. Below, the members hold up the standard of the Scuola di San Giovanni Evangelista, where the painting originated.

Michele di Matteo
(recorded in Bologna from 1410 to 1469)
4. *Saint Helena Polyptych*
Panels; the polyptych is made up of two orders separated by an overlying border 21 × 229 cm, and an overlying predella 38 × 229 cm. Each order is composed of three panels: 111 × 64 cm (upper middle), 142 × 63 cm (lower middle), and 11 × 85 cm (upper side), 142 × 85 cm (lower side).
Cat. 24
Acquisition: 1812, following the suppressions
Latest restoration: 2005

On the lower order is depicted the Virgin and Child with Four Angels; to the left, Saint Lucia and Saint Helena; to the right Mary Magdalene and Catherine of Alexandria; on the pendentives are four panels with the Doctors of the Church. On the band separating the two orders in sixteen nooks are the Redeemer and Saints. On the predella are five stories about the Discovery of the True Cross, from the left Saint Helena arrives in Jerusalem, Saint Helena convenes the Jews who keep counsel, Judas refuses to reveal where the Cross is, but after falling in a well he shows its location and he himself digs to find it,

Proof of the True Cross which revives a small boy, Adoration of the Cross while the devils flee. At Saint Catherine's feet is the almost illegible signature: "Michael Mathei da Bononia F." This comes from the church of Sant'Elena, where it was situated on the altar of the chapel of Saint Helena, erected in 1418 by Alessandro Borromei. The frame is from the original complex, but was restored in 1830. It is on the whole original, except for the pillars at the corners which have been lost. The work is considered one of the artist's masterpieces for the transparency of its

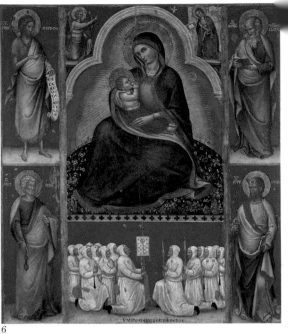

5 6

Veneto-Byzantine Painter from the Late-Thirteenth Century
7. *Madonna and Child*
Panel, gold ground, 77 × 38.5 cm
Cat. 884
Acquisition: 1932, from Burano cathedral
Latest restoration: 1939

Panel cropped at the sides, originally in Burano cathedral. It is generally associated with the *Nursing Virgin* in the Marciano Museum but reveals a more accentuated Byzantine component.

Jacobello Alberegno
(died before 1397)
8. *Christ on the Cross, between the Madonna and Saint John, Saints Gregory and Jerome*
Panel, gold ground, 40.5 × 55 cm
Cat. 25
Acquisition: 1816, from the bequest of Girolamo Molin
Latest restoration: 1939

Dated to around the 1380s. The Virgin and Saint John are depicted at three quarter face, giving depth to the gold ground.

The skull in the rocks at the foot of the cross is connected with and ancient Judeo-Christian cult for the burial of Abraham, a theme taken up often in seventeenth-century sculpture and fourteenth- and fifteenth-century Tuscan painting.

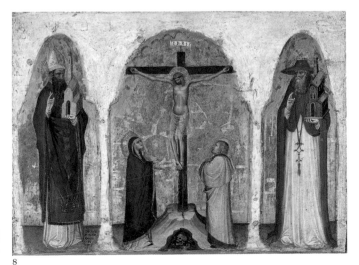

7 8

9

10

Lorenzo Veneziano
(recorded in Venice
from 1356 to 1372)
9. *The Annunciation and
Saints Gregory, John the
Baptist, James and Stephen*
Panels, gold ground,
111 × 55 cm (central),
94 × 24 cm (sides)
Cat. 9
Acquisition: 1812,
following the suppressions
Latest restoration: 1988

On the step of the throne
are the signature and the
date of 1371. The original
destination of the
gold-grounded work is
unknown. The use of the
flowery meadow constitutes
a new theme that would
be widely developed by
the International Gothic,
and used previously
by this artist in the panels
in the Staatliche Museen,
Berlin.

Lorenzo Veneziano
(recorded in Venice
from 1356 to 1372)
10. *Mystic Marriage
of Saint Catherine*
Panel, gold ground,
93 × 58 cm
Cat. 650
Acquisition: 1900, by
donation from the Udine
Seminary
Latest restoration: 1948

The artist's signature and
the date of February 2, 1359,
are visible below (according
to the *more veneto* dating
system and, therefore, really
1360). The original location
of the piece is unknown, but
it is believed to have been the
central part of a polyptych.
Once owned by the Marin
family in Venice, then it was
acquired by Jacopo Danieli,
passing on to Count
Pellegrino of Zara, then
to the Cernazai collection
and finally to the Udine
Seminary.

**Catarino di Marco
da Venezia**
(recorded in Venice
from 1362 to 1390)
11. *Coronation of the Virgin*
Panel, gold ground,
89 × 60.5 cm
Cat. 16
Acquisition: 1877, purchased
from Count Vincenzo Galli
Latest restoration: 1998

The work dates to 1375 and
depicts Jesus and the Virgin
seated on a single throne,
placed against a background
of the blue vault of heaven.
In spite of the use of the
same gestures and of rich
colors the work appears
less refined than Paolo
Veneziano's treatment
of the same subject.

Michele Giambono
(recorded from 1420 to 1462)
12. *Saint James the Elder and
Saint John the Evangelist,
the Blessed Filippo Benizzi,
Archangel Michael, and
Saint Louis of Toulouse*
Panel, gold ground,
108 × 45 cm (central),
88 × 29 cm (sides)
Cat. 3
Acquisition: 1812, following
the Napoleonic suppressions
Latest restoration: 1979

On the central part at the
bottom is written: "Michael /
Giambono pinxit." Acquired
in 1948 from the Scuola
del Cristo on the Giudecca
island, it originally
belonged to the church
of San Giacomo on the
Giudecca. The saint appears
in the central part and is
represented by the pilgrim's
staff and the book opened
to a part of the epistles
written to the apostle (I, 22),
while to his right stands
Filippo Benizzi, the founder
of the Serviti, with no halo
because he was only
canonized in 1671. Benizi
appears holding the book
of Psalms, opened to the
verse "Servus Tuus sum ego."
As a late work, datable
to around 1450, it suggests
an awareness, if not an
understanding, of the Tuscan
artists working in Venice,
especially Andrea del
Castagno, with his frescoes
in the chapel of San Tarasio
at San Zaccaria. At the
Albertina in Vienna there
is a drawing with variations
of Blessed Filippo and
Saint Michael.

11

12

Room 1

13

14

Jacobello del Fiore
(recorded in Venice
from 1401 to 1439)
13. *Madonna della
Misericordia, Saints John
the Baptist and John the
Evangelist, and the
Annunciation*
Panel, gold ground, with
gilded plaster decorations
87 × 114 cm
Cat. 13
Acquisition: 1816, from the
bequest of Girolamo Molin
Latest restoration: 1987

Its original location is
unknown. At the center are
the date and signature: "1436
Jachomello de Flor pense,"
which may also have been
written on the frame, now
lost. The date is clearly
incorrect, however, as it does
not correspond with the
stylistic nature of the piece.
Although the iconographical
motif of the *Platytera
Madonna* and the *Madonna
della Misericordia* together
was taken from Paolo
Veneziano, the painting
appears to owe more to the
influence of Gentile da
Fabriano and Michelino
da Besozzo. It is a variation
of a subject treated earlier, in
1407, on the Montegranaro
triptych (today in a private
collection in Switzerland).
Comparison with the
Montegranaro triptych
reveals a more subtle

elegance, less iconic fixedness
and even some studied
characterization of the small
worshippers kneeling in the
meadow covered with small
flowers. The work probably
dates to between 1415 and
1420. In fact, it bears a
similarity with the *Leone
Andante* in the Doge's Palace,
signed and dated 1415, and
was clearly painted before
the sumptuous *Justice
Triptych*, which is from 1421.
It is probable that the correct
transcription of the original
date must have been 1416.
With the removal of the
eighteenth-century frame,
some fragments were found
that had not been altered by
light or varnishes, and some
test brush marks.

**Venetian School from
the Fifteenth Century**
14. *The Cross of Saint
Theodore*
Rock crystal and partially
gilded silver, 92 × 43 cm,
bronze base 46 cm high
Cat. S 18
Acquisition: 1919, passed,
with the suppressions, into
the collection of Count
Savorgnan, then to Abbot
Luigi Celotti who sold it
to the Emperor of Austria
for the new Imperial Museum
in Vienna. It was assigned
to the Galleries with the
post-war restitutions of 1919
Latest restoration: 2007

Originally in the Scuola
Grande di San Teodoro.
Executed in rock crystal
and partly gilt silver, the
cross is set in a display case,
made by Carlo Scarpa from
glass, iron and a fragment
of ancient porphyry.
It reflects the important
innovations by Tuscan artists
working in Venice, while
retaining Gothic elements
from Northern Europe.
The bronze base, attributed
to Alessandro Vittoria, dates
from 1567, as can be read
in the inscription running
round three sides.

Jacobello Alberegno
(died before 1397)
15. *Polyptych of the
Apocalypse*
(*Vision of Saint John the
Evangelist on Patmos,
Harvest and Vintage of the
Angels of the Lord, the Whore
of Babylon on the Beast of the
Apocalypse, the Cavalcade
of Kings, Last Judgment*)
Panel, gold ground
95 × 61 cm (central),
45 × 32 cm, 45 × 33 cm,
44 × 33 cm, 45 × 32 cm (sides)
Cat. 1000
Acquisition: 1951,
became State property
after the suppressions. Five
panels moved to the
depository of San Giovanni
Evangelista from where, in
1838, the *Vision* and the
Judgment were sent on to

Vienna and then returned
with the post-war
restitutions of 1919.
Displayed in the Museum on
Torcello until 1948. In that
year they were reunited with
the others which, since 1840,
had been in the Correr
Museum. Finally, in 1951,
the whole group came
to the Accademia Galleries
Latest restoration: 1952

The five panels depict one of
the visions described by Saint
John in the *Apocalypse*, with
the steps marked by Roman
numerals. The central panel
shows Eternity in Glory, with
the lamb between the four
symbols of the Evangelists
(IV), with "six wings [...] and
full of eyes," adored by
twenty-four elders; the side
panels depict the Harvest of
the Earth (XIV): "thrust in
thy sickle, and reap: for the
time is come for thee to reap;
for the harvest of the earth is
ripe" (14, 5–16, 1); Babylon
(XVII), or "the great whore
[...] seated atop a beast [...]
with seven heads and ten
horns" (16, 2–17, 8); the
Cavalcade of the Kings
(XIX): "And behold a white
horse; horse and he who sat
upon him [...] on his head
were many crowns; and the
armies which were in heaven
followed him upon white
horses" (18, 18–19, 21) and
the Final Judgment (XX):

15

"I saw a great white throne and him that sat on it [...] And I saw the dead, small and great, stand before God; and the books were opened [...]" (20, 11 00, 5).
On the book that Christ holds open is written: "chi no / n è scri / ti.su / questo / libro // sera da / nadi."
Originally the work was housed in the church of San Giovanni Evangelista on Torcello, which fell into ruin over the course of only a few decades until it was demolished. The complex allegorical theme performs its didactic function with great clarity, while the figurative culture of Giusto de' Menabuoi is transposed in the more typically Venetian terms of chromatic sensibility and expressive strength. The church of San Giovanni Evangelista on Torcello was reconstructed after a fire in 1342, providing us with a *post quem* date for the work sometime in the latter half of that century.

**Venetian School
of the Second Half
of the Fourteenth Century**
16. *Coronation of the Virgin
and the Stories of Christ*
Panel, gold ground,
55 × 39 cm (central),
55 × 41 cm (sides)
Cat. 23, 4a, b, c, d
Acquisition. 1816, from the bequest of Girolamo Molin, *Coronation of the Virgin, Descent from the Cross, Resurrection, Ascension, Pentecoste* (the other four *Stories—Nativity, Christ with the Doctors*, the *Last Supper*, the *Crucifixion*—on deposit from the Correr Museum)
Latest restoration: 1951–54
At the center, the Coronation of the Virgin; at the sides, the Stories of Christ: the Nativity, Christ with the Doctors, the Last Supper, the Crucifixion, the Deposition, the Resurrection, the Ascension and the Pentecost. The paintings are part of a single group of unknown origin which had been separated and was reassembled in 1954.

16

17

Catarino di Marco da Venezia
(recorded from 1362 to 1390)
(documented in Venice
from 1362 to 1390)
17. *Coronation of the Virgin
and Saints Lucy and
Nicholas of Tolentino*
Panel, gold ground,
105 × 58 cm (central),
96 × 28 cm (sides)
Cat. 702
Acquisition: 1902, purchase
of Tommaso Mazzoli
Latest restoration: 1951

The original location of the
triptych is unknown, but
it was probably painted later
than the *Coronation of the
Virgin* (Room 1, cat. 16)
of 1375 as is borne out by
the nonchalance of the
figures, the elegance
of Saint Lucy, inspired
by Lorenzo Veneziano,
and the rough features
of Saint Nicholas.

**Stefano "Plebanus"
di Sant'Agnese**
(recorded from 1369 to 1385)
18. *Coronation of the Virgin*
Panel, gold ground,
75 × 52 cm
Cat. 21/A
Acquisition: 1816, from the
bequest of Girolamo Molin
Latest restoration: 1951

The painting is signed and
dated 1381: "MCCCLXXXI /
STEFAN / PLEBANUS / SCE /
AGNET / PINXIT" ("plebanus"
means parishioner).
Although the work is based
on the *Coronation of the
Virgin* by Paolo Veneziano,
here it is read with a full
Gothic sensitivity, evident
in the play of the perspective
planes and the use of light
and brilliant colors.

18

Antonio Vivarini
(Murano ca. 1418/20–
Venice 1476/84)
19. *Virgin and Child*
Panel, gold ground,
64 × 41 cm
Cat. 1236
Acquisition: 1959, from
the parish of San Giorgio
delle Pertiche where it had
been deposited since 1846
Latest restoration: 1958–59

The original location of this
devotional panel is unknown.
However, since it came
from State holdings it must
once have been housed
in a public building, a theory
also supported by a 1711
inscription on the back
of the piece which refers
to a magistracy during which
time the work was probably
restored. The painting
is extremely contained,
and in spite of the retention
of the gold ground it reveals
a knowledge of new research
on volume and bright colors,
techniques proposed by the
Tuscans, and particularly
Masolino. It dates to about
1440.

**Veneto School of the Late
Fourteenth–Early Fifteenth
Century**
20. *Portable Altar*
Panel, 119.5 × 45 cm (central),
119.5 × 40 cm (sides)
Cat. 14
Acquisition: 1812,
following the suppressions
Latest restoration: 2007

On the central panel:
Madonna of Humility;
above: Pietà; at the sides:
Saints James and Francis.
The backs of the side panels
represent the instruments
of the Passion. The work,
which comes from the church
of San Gregorio, has been
attributed to the Master
of the Giovannelli Madonna,
doubtfully identified as
Francesco del Fiore, father
of the more celebrated
Jacobello.

Nicolò di Pietro
(recorded in Venice from
1394 to 1427)
21. *Saint Lawrence*
Panel, gold ground,
63 × 23 cm
Cat. 20
Acquisition: 1816, from the
bequest of Girolamo Molin
Latest restoration: 1951

Probably part of a lost
polyptych, the panel is placed
towards the later phase
of the artist's working-life.

19

20

21

Room 1

22

23

Nicolò di Pietro
(recorded in Venice
from 1394 to 1427)
22. *Madonna and Child
Enthroned with Musician
Angels and the Donor
Vulciano Belgarzone di Zara*
Panel, gold ground,
107 × 66 cm
Cat. 19
Acquisition: 1856, by
purchase from the Manfrini
collection
Latest restoration: 1949

Under the footboard of the
throne is written: "hoc / opus
/ fecit fiei / dns vulcia /
belgarcone / civis.ya /
driensis / MCCCLXXXXIIII.
Nichola / filus mri Petri
pictoris de vene / ciis pinxit
hoc opus qui mo / ratur in
chapite pontis paradixi,"
which denotes the date
of 1394, the name of the
commissioner, the artist's
signature and his address
at the foot of the Paradiso
bridge.
The earliest signed and dated
work by Nicolò, the panel
is so cohesive and refined

that the question regarding
the artist's previous training
and production has not yet
been fully answered, nor has
his role during the transition
from Venetian painting
of the fourteenth century
to that of the fifteenth been
adequately understood.
Compared with the abstract
nature of Paolo Veneziano,
the chromatic refinement of
Lorenzo, the decorativeness
of Jacobello, Nicolò is
characterized by a new
coloring and volume. Rather
than Bohemian figurative
models, as is often repeated,
he is notable for an acute
interest in the culture
of mainland Italy, from
the works of Altichiero
and Avanzo to the frescoes
in Treviso by Tommaso
da Modena, and the works
of Vitale da Bologna and
other of his contemporaries
in Bologna.

Antonio Vivarini
(Murano ca. 1418/20–
Venice 1476/84)
23. *Marriage of Saint
Monica*
Panel, gold ground,
46.5 × 31.5 cm
Cat. 50
Acquisition: 1816, from the
bequest of Girolamo Molin
Latest restoration: 1951

Dated to around 1441, the
panel was part of a series
of Stories placed around
a statue of Saint Monica in
the church of Santo Stefano.
Below, a caption explains the
depiction: "qui è como sancta
Monika fu mandata a marito
dal padre e da la madre"
("here it is shown how Saint
Monica was sent to marriage
by her father and mother").
Inspired by the style of
Masolino and Paolo Uccello,
the scene reveals new
elements from the customs
of the time and a studied
use of perspective.

Michele Giambono
(recorded from 1420 to 1462)
24. *Coronation of the Virgin
in Heaven*
Panel, gold ground,
with gilded plaster
decorations, 228 × 177 cm
Cat. 33
Acquisition: 1816, from the
bequest of Girolamo Molin
Latest restoration: 1949

Probably painted for the
church of Sant'Agnese
around the middle of the
fifteenth century, the panel
repeats the same scheme
and subject as that
of Antonio Vivarini and
Giovanni d'Alemagna
at the church of San
Pantalon. Beneath the throne
are putti who hold up the
instruments of the Passion,
while below them are the
Evangelists flanked by the
four Doctors of the Church.
The surrounding space is
entirely occupied by saints
and orders of angels.

24

25

Lorenzo Veneziano
(recorded in Venice
from 1356 to 1372)
25. *Polyptych with
the Annunciation
(Lion Polyptych)*
Panel, gold ground, lower
order: 126 × 75 cm (central),
121 × 60 cm (sides);

upper order: 82 × 83 cm
(central), 67 × 30 cm
(eight sides), 35 × 5 cm
(36 small panels on the
pillars)
Cat. 10
Acquisition: 1812,
following the suppressions
Latest restoration: 1997

At left, Saints Anthony
(Abbot), John the Baptist,
Paul and Peter. At right,
Saints John the Evangelist,
Magdalene, Dominic and
Francis. On the upper order,
the Holy Father giving his
blessing among eight
Prophets. Below, on the

predella, are the Hermit
Saints Saba, Macarius, Paul,
Hilary and Theodore. A work
of very fine artistic quality,
it was originally on the high
altar of the now demolished
church of Sant'Antonio in
Castello. On the inscription
on the tablets at the sides

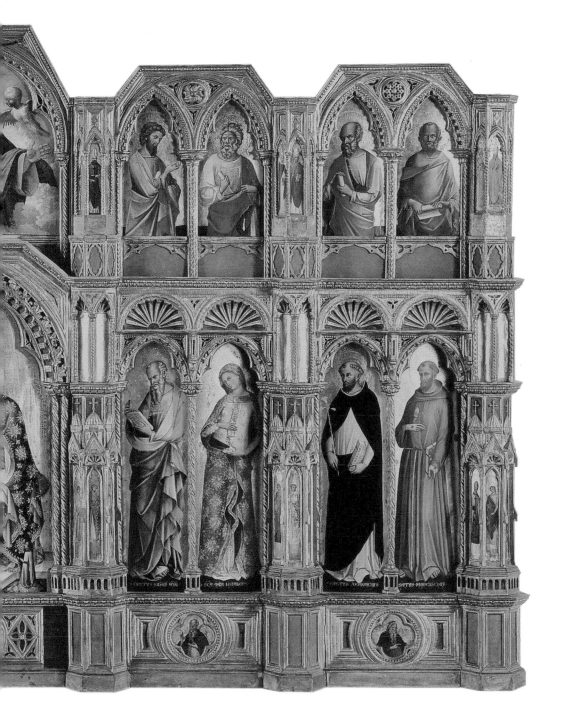

of the central panel are written the date when the work was begun (1357), the name of the painter Lorenzo, the engraver of the frame Zanino and the dedication to the commissioner Domenico Lion, shown to the lower right of the Virgin.

The lower order—with its great Gothic elegance—is arranged according to a chromatic crescendo which begins with the dark tones of the side figures of Saint Anthony and Saint Francis and gradually reaches full chromatic

luminosity n the central scene of the Annunciation. The highly unusual iconography for the central section was most likely requested by Lion. The upper panel in the center is a replacement of the original, which

was lost, and is possibly the work of Benedetto Diana (Venice ca. 1460–1525).

Room 1

26

Giovanni Baronzio, attr.
(recorded in Rimini 1343
to 1345)
26. *Stories from the Passion
of Christ and the Last
Judgment*
Panel, gold ground,
17 × 15 cm each
Cat. 26
Acquisition: 1816, from the
bequest of Girolamo Molin
Latest restoration: 1979

These five panels: *Stories
of the Passion of Christ* (*Kiss
of Judas, Condemnation
of Christ*, the *Deposition,
Crucifixion, Deposition
from the Cross*) and the
Last Judgment belonged
to the same group, together
with the five panels of
identical format in the
Staatliche Museen, Berlin,
and a *Deposition in the Tomb*
in a private collection
in Rome. The panels were
probably the doors of a
private devotional diptych
with the *Stories* distributed

on three registers. More
recently, the complex has
been attributed to Giovanni
Baronzio's early period.

**Master of Ceneda
(Ercole del Fiore?)**
(recorded from 1439 to 1484)
27. *Coronation of the Virgin
in Paradise with Donor*
Panel, gold ground,
281 × 302 cm
Cat. 1
Acquisition: 1882, by
purchase from the Duomo
of Ceneda
Latest restoration: 2006–07

Dating from the first half
of the fifteenth century,
the work was commissioned
for the high altar of the
cathedral of Ceneda by the
city's bishop Antonio Correr
(portrayed kneeling at the
bottom right) on the
completion of the rebuilding
of the church begun
in about 1432. The crowded
composition presents

a more complex version
of the *Paradise* by Guariento
at the Ducal Palace.

Jacopo Moranzone
(recorded from 1430;
died between 1467 and 1469)
28. *Assumption of the Virgin
and Saints Helena, John
the Baptist, Benedict and
Elizabeth*
Panel, gold ground,
135 × 59 cm (central),
124 × 32 cm (sides)
Cat. 11
Acquisition: 1812,
following the suppressions
Latest restoration: 1952

On the central panel the
Assumption; on the side
panels Saints Helen,
John the Baptist, Benedict
and Elizabeth.
Originally in the church
of Sant'Elena, where it
was painted with part
of a bequest established
in 1441 by Donna Elisabetta,
the mother of Fra' Tommaso

da Venezia. Sources indicate
a possible inscription with
the date of 1441, perhaps
on the now lost wooden
frame. Cited by Vasari in
1568 as the only work worthy
of mention by the artist,
who "made all his figures
on the points of their feet."
The Gothic-like composition,
influenced by Michele di
Matteo's polyptych for the
same church of Sant'Elena,
indicates that the artist
is barely aware of the new
artistic ideas being developed
in Venice at that time, while
certain roughness around
the edges reveal an aspect
typical in engraving, which
was an age old tradition
in the Moranzone family.

27

28

2 Giovanni Bellini and Great Fifteenth-Century Altarpieces

This room was built between 1886 and 1895 to house Titian's *Assumption* and other large altarpieces. After the *Assumption* was returned to the church of the Frari in 1919, the room appeared rather out of balance. To restore its harmony, in 1951 Carlo Scarpa replaced the decorated ceiling with dark green plaster, replaced the polychrome marble floor with a dark grey Venetian style "terrazzo," concealed the entrance with a large masonry panel and installed a new flight of stairs to Room 3.

Giovanni Bellini
Madonna and Child Enthroned with Saints Francis, John the Baptist, Job, Dominic, Sebastian, Louis of Toulouse and Angels (San Giobbe Altarpiece), detail.

Vittore Carpaccio
(Venice ca. 1460–
before June 1526)
1. *Crucifixion and the
Apotheosis of the 10,000
Martyrs of Mount Ararat*
Canvas, 311 × 204 cm
Cat. 89
Acquisition: 1812,
following the suppressions
Latest restoration: 2006,
financed by Rona Goffen

Signed and dated 1515, this
altarpiece was painted for
the Ottobon altar in the
demolished church of
Sant'Antonio di Castello,
of whose structure there
remains a trace at the sides,
in the outlines of the bases
and the capitals. It was
probably commissioned by
Ettore Ottobon, nephew of
the prior Francesco Ottobon,
who had halted an outbreak
of plague in his monastery
by the intercession of the ten
thousand martyrs of Mount
Ararat. The legend recounts
that nine thousand Roman
soldiers, led by Acatius, were
sent against the Armenian
rebels and succeeded in
defeating them only after
imploring the help of Jesus
at the suggestion of an angel.
The angel then led them
to Mount Ararat, where
he instructed them in the
Christian religion. On
learning of their conversion,
the emperor reached them
with another pagan king,
threatening to inflict on
them all the pains endured
by Christ crucified. Their
firm faith, even under
torture, converted another
thousand pagan soldiers,
who joined them. During
a violent thunderstorm
came the final passion,
like that of Jesus.
The altarpiece contains
various echoes of the most
recent artistic developments
of the day, including the
influence of the woodcut
and painting by Dürer
of the same subject in the
Kunsthistorisches Museum
of Vienna. Despite a certain
compositional virtuosity,
based on a careful
preparatory drawing revealed
by infrared-ray analysis, it
constitutes an extraordinary
innovation in the field of
Venetian religious painting.
It replaces the usual votive
representation of one saint or
a small group with a plurality
of images, so presenting
a collective example
of Christian virtue.

Marco Basaiti
(Venice 1470/75–post 1530)
2. *Prayer in the Garden with
Saints Louis of Toulouse,
Francis, Dominic and Mark*
Canvas for transport
from a panel, 369 × 222 cm
Cat. 69
Acquisition: 1815, from
the church of San Giobbe
Latest restoration: 1987

At the foreground to the left
on the ground is the
fragmentary signature
and the date of 1510. The
altarpiece was originally
in the church of San Giobbe,
on the first altar to the right
belonging to the Foscari
family. The composition
follows a pyramidal scheme:
the evangelical event takes
place beyond the arc,
while at the front are
the eponymous saints
of the Foscari family—Louis
of Toulouse) and Francis
to the left, Dominic and
Mark to the right—presented
as intermediaries between
the faithful and the
divinity.

1

2

3

Giovanni Bellini
(Venice 1434/39–1516)
*3. Madonna and Child
Enthroned with Saints
Francis, John the Baptist,
Job, Dominic, Sebastian,
Louis of Toulouse and Angels*
(*San Giobbe Altarpiece*)
Panel, 471 × 292 cm
Cat. 38
Acquisition: 1815, from the
church of San Giobbe
Latest restoration: 1994–95
and 2004

Originally in the church
of San Giobbe on the altar
of Saint Job, the second one
to the right. The large panel
received great admiration
from other artists at the time
of its creation, and became
a model for successive
altarpieces. It has been
shortened by 50 centimeters
at the top. The presence
of the apotropaic saints
Sebastian and Job indicates
that the altarpiece was
painted during a plague,

probably the one of 1478.
The niche, with its naturally
proportioned figures
composed in a pyramid,
is almost a symbolic
representation of the
San Marco Basilica: the
apse with the gilt mosaics,
the stone wall paneling,
the seraphs, all allude to the
Basilica. The triads of saints
to the left and right of the
Madonna are arranged
in triangular patterns.
In its original location,

the illusion of depth was
accentuated by sculpted
pilaster strips on the altar,
faithful repetitions of those
painted on the piece.
The angels in the lower
area playing the lute
and the lyre are in honor
of Saint Job, the patron
saint of music.

Room 2

4

Vittore Carpaccio
(Venice ca. 1460–
before June 1526)
4. *Presentation of Christ
in the Temple*
Panel, 420 × 231 cm
Cat. 44
Acquisition: 1815, from the
church of San Giobbe
Latest restoration: 1995

Signed and dated 1510, the altarpiece was originally in the church of San Giobbe in the third altar on the right (dedicated to the Purification of the Virgin), and was probably commissioned by Pietro di Matteo Sanudo. The presentation of the infant Jesus in the temple—forty days after his birth—occurs in a space in the shape of an apse, whereas the figures are all composed in a pyramidal arrangement. In addition to the exceptional chromatic quality—recovered with the most recent restoration—certain aspects deserve emphasizing: the female faces inspired by the works of Pietro Perugino; the scenes from Genesis and the Apocalypse decorating the clothes of Simon, the priest; the three angels at the base playing the lute, lyre and cromocorno. Considered to be a preparatory study for the two women's heads to the left of the Virgin, is a drawing in the Ashmolean Museum, Oxford, which was also used for the *Apotheosis of Saint Ursula* (Room 21, cat. 576).

5

Giambattista Cima da Conegliano
(Conegliano 1459/60–1517/18)
5. *Madonna and Child
with Saints Jerome and
Louis of Toulouse*
(*Madonna of the Orange Tree*)
Panel, 211 × 139 cm
Cat. 815
Acquisition: 1919, returned
from Austria
Latest restoration: 1995

This signed altarpiece
was originally to the right
of the high altar in the
church of Santa Chiara
on Murano, and belonged
to Franciscan monks. The
presence of the Franciscan
Saint Louis of Toulouse, and
the two monks about to enter
the woods suggest that
the work was commissioned
by the same order. The

theme is a variation on
the "Flight into Egypt,"
an allusion provided by
Saint Joseph and the ass
in the background. The
sacra conversazione thus
takes place in a wide
landscape, where certain
symbols of Mary can be
recognized, such as the city
on the hill which recalls
the birthplace of the artist,

and rock which is also Mary's
throne, and the orange tree
after which the painting
was named. A preparatory
drawing for the head
of Saint Jerome is kept at the
British Museum in London.
The work dates to between
1496 and 1498.

Room 2

6

7

Giambattista Cima da Conegliano
(Conegliano 1459/60–1517/18)
6. *Virgin and Child Enthroned with Saints Catherine (?), George, Nicholas, Anthony Abbot, Sebastian and Lucy (?)* (*Dragan Altarpiece*)
Panel, 412 × 210 cm
Cat. 36
Acquisition: 1812, following the suppressions
Latest restoration: 2004–05

From the chapel of San Gregorio in the church of Santa Maria della Carità. According to sources, the marble frame had been commissioned from Cristoforo Solari of Milan by Giorgio Dragan, a Venetian sea-captain, probably depicted in the features of Saint George. In the original location, the painting most likely presented a strong spatial affinity between its painted architectural elements and the architectural structures of the altar. The work must have been completed in around 1499, the date of the commissioner's death and of a very similar polyptych by Miglionico.

Giambattista Cima da Conegliano
(Conegliano 1459/60–1517/18)
7. *Doubting Thomas with Saint Magnus, Bishop of Oderzo*
Panel, 210 × 141 cm
Cat. 611
Acquisition: 1829, following the suppressions
Latest restoration: 1998

From the Scuola dei Mureri (masons) at San Samuele, with the Scuola's patrons, the Saints Thomas and Magnus the Bishop, also depicted. The work dates to around 1504–05, immediately after the London version of the same subject, carried out originally for a confraternity in Portogruaro between 1502 and 1504. The episode does not unfold in an enclosed space, as the evangelical tradition would normally have it, but in an open loggia, with Saint Magnus taking the place of the usual eleven apostles. The careful use of shadows and light and the remarkable compositional balance make this one of the most important of the artist's works of that time.

8

9

**Giovanni Bellini
and Assistants**
(Venice 1434/39–1516)
8. *Mourning the Dead Christ*
Canvas, 445 × 310 cm
Cat. 166
Acquisition: 1829, following
the Napoleonic suppressions
Latest restoration: 1964

Originally in the now
demolished church
of Santa Maria dei Servi
on one of the first altars
to the right, demolished in
1510 and reconstructed at the
expense of the Servite friars.
The painting also dates to
about that time, and its
very high quality—in spite
of a previous attribution

to Rocco Marconi—suggests
that Bellini was largely
responsible for the piece,
with only limited
intervention from his
assistants. Saint Joseph
of Arimathea, the Virgin
and the Magdalen are
recognizable, but it is harder
to identify the two figures
at the ends. Previously
thought to be Saint Martha
and Philip Benizzi,
it has been suggested
more recently that they
are Juliana Falconieri
and Bonaventure of Forlì.

Marco Basaiti
(Venice 1470/75–post 1530)
9. *Vocation of the Sons
of Zebedee*
Panel, 385 × 265 cm
Cat. 39
Acquisition: 1812, following
the Napoleonic suppressions
Latest restoration: 1990–91

Signed and dated "Marco
Basaiti 1510," the work was
once on the high altar of the
church of Sant'Andrea della
Certosa. The most recent
restoration revealed that
the altarpiece was enlarged
when the work was almost
complete with the addition
of the boats and the
fisherman (Mark 1, 16–20),

also with some corrections
to the large figures
in the foreground and
to the background.
The work was probably
begun by Alvise Vivarini,
but when this master died
it was taken over and
completed by Marco Basaiti,
who worked in Vivarini's
workshop at that time.
The evangelical theme
of the "calling" is a clear
reference to monastic life,
also alluded to in various
other symbolic motifs
in the composition.

Room 2

3 Giovanni Bellini, Giorgione, Cima da Conegliano, Sebastiano del Piombo and Benedetto Diana

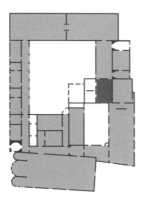

This room was originally part of the ancient hospital of the Scuola della Carità. It was also called the "Saletta di Canova" because it once held the porphyry urn containing his right hand, which was then placed in the tablinum and finally moved to the parish church of Possagno in 2008. The window frames were designed by Carlo Scarpa, probably when he planned the arrangement of the displays in the adjoining rooms.

**Giovanni Bellini
and Assistants**
The Virgin Annunciate, detail.

1

2

Sebastiano Luciani known as Sebastiano del Piombo
(Venice 1485–Rome 1547)
1. *Saints Louis of Toulouse, Sinibald, Bartholomew and Sebastian*
Canvas, 292 × 137 cm, 292 × 137 cm, 292 × 136 cm, 292 × 136 cm
Latest restoration: 1984–85

These are the outer and inner doors from an organ (today destroyed) formerly in the church of San

Bartolomeo, on deposit with the Gallery. Inspired by Giovanni Bellini and above all Giorgione, they were painted in about 1508–09, or more likely 1510–11, as scholars have recently shown, noting their morphological closeness to the artist's first works from the Roman period. They are the most important of his early commissions.

Giambattista Cima da Conegliano
(Conegliano 1459/60–1517/18)
2. *Madonna and Child between Saints John the Baptist and Paul*
Panel, 82 × 114 cm
Cat. 603
Acquisition: 1838, by donation from Girolamo Contarini
Latest restoration: 2005

Dates from the early sixteenth century. The face of the Virgin already reveals the typical characteristics of Cima's style, although the influence of Giovanni Bellini is still quite strong.

3

**Giovanni Bellini
and Assistants**
(Venice 1434/39–1516)
3. *The Angel of the
Annunciation,
The Virgin Annunciate*
and *Saint Peter*
Canvas, 225 × 105 cm each
Cat. 734
Acquisition: 1907,
*The Angel of the
Annunciation*, by purchase;
1910, *The Virgin
Annunciate*, withdrawn from
the depository of San
Francesco della Vigna; 1908,
Saint Peter withdrawn from
the depository of the church
of the Frari
Latest restoration: 1998

The two paintings,
representing the Angel
of the Annunciation and the
Virgin Annunciate, originally
decorated the external doors
of the organ of Santa Maria
dei Miracoli; the internal
doors had Saint Peter and a
Saint Paul (lost). The three
canvases have been attributed
to various artists, including
Carpaccio, as an external
reference to the *Dream of
Ursula*; today it is believed to
have been the work of some
artists working in the style of
Giovanni Bellini, and based
on drawings by the master.
The marble pieces
in the paintings recall those
of the interior of the Miracoli
church, which was completed
in 1489. This date signals
the *post quem* period
for the date of the paintings,
which are probably from the
last decade of that century.

3

Room 3

4

**Giambattista Cima
da Conegliano**
(Conegliano 1459/60–
1517/18)
4. *Lamentation over the
Dead Christ Supported
by the Virgin, Nicodemus,
Saint John the Evangelist
and the Marys*
(*Pietà*)
Panel, 70 × 113 cm
Cat. 604
Acquisition: 1850, from the
bequest of Felicita Renier
Latest restoration: 2005

Signed bottom-right, the
piece appears to be from
the younger period of the
artist's life (around 1490),
as it has no landscape details
whatsoever. The many
allusions to Alvise Vivarini,
Antonello and Giovanni
Bellini combine to create
a piece of great balance.

5

**Sebastiano Luciani known as
Sebastiano del Piombo,
attr.**
(Venice 1485–Rome 1547)
5. *Virgin and Child with
Saints Catherine and John
the Baptist*
Panel, 51 × 80 cm
Cat. 70
Acquisition: 1838, by
donation from Girolamo
Contarini
Latest restoration: 2002

From the Contarini
collection, the piece may

have been commissioned by
a certain Caterina Contarini,
as the inclusion of Saint
Catherine would indicate.
Although critics are divided
as to whether the painting
is by Sebastiano del Piombo
or by Giorgione (or one
of his followers), the
style of the painting
recalls the early efforts
of Sebastiano, characterized
by the influence of Giovanni
Bellini and the modern
"language" employed
by Giorgione.

6

7

Benedetto Rusconi known as Benedetto Diana
(Venice ca. 1460–1525)
6. *Virgin and Child with the Infant Saint John, between Saints Louis of Toulouse and Monica*
Panel, 180 × 152 cm
Cat. 86
Acquisition: 1832, probably following the suppressions
Latest restoration: 1979

Originally on the altar of the sacristy in the church of Maria dei Servi, where it was placed upon a lunette with the Holy Father, identified by some as the one set at the top of the large polyptych by Lorenzo Veneziano (Room 1, cat. 10). It is a late work from around 1520, when the influence of Giorgione was enriched by experience with contemporary Lombard painting.

Giorgio or Zorzi da Castelfranco known as Giorgione
(Castelfranco 1476/77– Venice 1510)
7. *Nude*
Detached fresco,
243 × 140 cm
Cat. 1034
Acquisition: 1937, from the top story of the Fondaco dei Tedeschi, front facing onto the Grand Canal
Latest restoration: 1977

The fragment of the feminine figure usually defined "Nude," but in reality allegorical figure holding in hand a sphere, comes from the façade of the Fondaco dei Tedeschi, completed by Giorgione in 1508. It was part of a wide decoration which developed a complex iconographical program, already unclear to Vasari (1568). In spite of the precarious state of conservation, it is possible to recognize the marks of the deep original tone.

Room 3

4/5 Currently closed for restoration

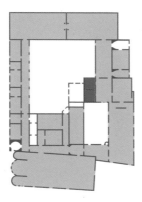

Carlo Scarpa redesigned these two rooms (4 and 5) in 1955, walling over their windows and making them into one open space divided at the center in correspondence with the two pre-existing skylights.
Works were shown using only original frames or frames of the same era; paintings lacking a frame were inserted into wooden panels lined with material. For Giorgione's *Tempest* brown velvet was used.
The works have been temporarily installed in Room 13.

6 Titian, Jacopo Tintoretto and Paolo Veronese

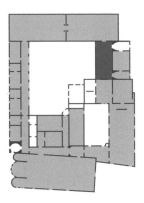

Part of the "Nuovissima" (very new) wing connecting the old Scuola with Rooms 10 and 11, this room and the neighboring rooms were built between 1840 and 1857. For a long time this was one of the poorest rooms in the Galleries, but in 1988, when the exhibition was held of Paolo Veronese's restored works, it was here that some of his great ceiling paintings were housed. Two walled-up windows facing onto the courtyard by Andrea Palladio were reopened over the course of 2000.

Titian
Saint John the Baptist, detail.

1

Tiziano Vecellio known as Titian
(Pieve di Cadore
ca. 1488/90–Venice 1576)
1. *Saint John the Baptist*
Canvas, 201 × 119 cm
Cat. 314
Acquisition: 1808,
following the suppressions
Latest restoration: 1981

Signed "Ticianus" on the stone at the bottom, this painting was originally located in the church of Santa Maria Maggiore and after strong protest from the Venetians, the piece was entrusted to the Accademia Galleries rather than being transferred to the Brera Gallery in Milan. The work follows a precise figurative

program in which "drawing," "color" and "invention" are merged—almost a response to the Tuscan debate about whether Venetian artists were capable of drawing well. The figure of the saint— whose stunning preparatory sketch has been revealed by the reflectography—recalls both Michelangelo and classical art sources, while

the background landscape is decidedly fresh and new. The work is from around the time of the *Presentation of Mary at the Temple* (Room 24, cat. 626), and the *Christ Crowned with Thorns* in the Louvre, which date to 1540.

2

Tiziano Vecellio known as Titian
(Pieve di Cadore
ca. 1480/90–Venice 1576)
2. *Virgin and Child*
Canvas, 124 × 96 cm
Cat. 1359
Acquisition: 1981, from
the bequest of Leonardo
Albertini
Latest restoration: 2005
(maintenance)

For private devotion, this
painting belonged to the
Mazenta Marquises of Milan,
at least from 1616 until 1879,
when it passed to the Pinetti
Martinengo family of
Bergamo. It was purchased
in 1916 by Luigi Albertini,
father of Leonardo.
To the left of the composition
can be seen the burning

bush, symbol of the eternal
virginity of Mary. X-rays
have revealed that the
artist used a canvas for this
painting on which he had
previously painted a praying
saint. From about 1560.

Room 6

3

Jacopo Robusti known as Jacopo Tintoretto
(Venice 1519–1594)
3. *Creation of the Animals*
4. *Temptation of Adam and Eve*
5. *Cain and Abel*
Canvases, 150 × 258 cm,
150 × 220 cm, 149 × 196 cm
Cats. 900, 43, 41
Acquisition: 1928, *Creation of the Animals* from the depository of the Doge's Palace; 1812, the other two canvases, following the suppressions
Latest restoration: 1967

These three works were created between 1550 and 1553 and were originally in the Scuola della Trinità, a school instituted by the Teutonic Knights near the Dogana da Mar, which was demolished in the 1600s for the construction of the Salute Basilica and rebuilt nearby. There were originally five paintings with the *Stories of Genesis* which were to complete the decoration of the Sala dell'Albergo, begun by Francesco Torbido. Of the five canvases by Tintoretto in addition to these, there is a fragment with *Adam and Eve before the Holy Father* at the Uffizi in Florence. On the *Creation*, the articulate forms of the other two stories becomes a painting composed almost like a tapestry, where a single vital breath seems to animate the Creator and his creatures. On the *Adam and Eve*, the nude bodies—arranged diagonally according to a refined mannerist technique—rake against the dense mass of foliage. Adam and Eve are captured just before the consummation of their sin; to the right the sin has already been committed and the two progenitors are chased out by the angel. This is a fundamental work for the artist's treatment of landscapes. Also on *Cain and Abel* the figures are depicted against dense vegetation, which opens to the right onto an remarkable piece of landscape, with the minuscule figure of Cain wandering in the distance. The subject recalls a similar painting by Andrea Schiavone in the Galleria Palatina in Florence, and especially the Titian painting of the ceiling of Santo Spirito in Isola, later transferred to the sacristy of the Salute Basilica.

4

5

6

7

Jacopo Robusti known as Jacopo Tintoretto
(Venice 1519–1594)
6. *Saint Louis of Toulouse, Saint George and the Princess*
Canvas, 230 × 150 cm
Cat. 899
Acquisition: 1937, from the Ante-Chiesetta Room at the Doge's Palace where it had been stored
Latest restoration: 1986

Like the *Saints Andrew and Jerome*, this work was created for the first room of the Salt Magistrate in the Palazzo Camerlenghi at the Rialto, and was commissioned by the magistrates Giorgio Venier and Alvise Foscarini who, upon completion of their service on September 13,

1551, and May 1, 1552, offered a votive painting for their office. The work was completed around 1552. On the composition, with its anti-conformist and unusual iconography, the female figure ardently rides the dragon in a posture of great virtuosity, turned round towards the back and towards the saviour, mirroring herself in his shiny breastplate. Saint Louis of Toulouse's pensive aspect comprises a very effective scene. Tintoretto probably had some contact with contemporary theater, and it may even be the case that he took inspiration from the set of Aretino's *Talanta*, drawn by Vasari around 1542.

Jacopo Robusti known as Jacopo Tintoretto
(Venice 1519–1594)
7. *Saints Andrew and Jerome*
Canvas, 230 × 150 cm
Cat. 898
Acquisition: 1937, from the Ante-Chiesetta Room at the Doge's Palace, where it had been stored
Latest restoration: 1986

Commissioned by the magistrates Andrea Dandolo and Girolamo Bernardo, who completed their service on September 6, 1552, and October 9, 1552. This last date provides us with a *post quem* date for the completion of the work, which was painted shortly after *Saint Louis of Toulouse, Saint George and the Princess*.

The large Cross painted transversally between the two nude bodies of the saints creates the optical illusion of extraordinary depth.

8

Paolo Caliari known as Paolo Veronese
(Verona 1528–Venice 1588)
8. *Venice Receiving Gifts from Hercules and Ceres*
Canvas, 308 × 327 cm
Cat. 45
Acquisition: 1895,
from Palazzo Reale
Latest restoration: 1986

Originally on the ceiling of the Corn Magistrate's Room in the Doge's Palace, in 1792 it was brought to the Marciana Library. In 1810 it was moved to the ceiling of the Napoleonic wing, and then later to the Accademia. The format of the painting, perhaps rectangular originally, was altered, probably in conjunction with its first transfer. It dates to around the same time as the canvases in the Collegio Room of the Doge's Palace, and especially *Venice between Justice and Peace* of 1576–78. A fundamental work of the artist for its crafted use of perspective and counter-lighting and its chromatic refinement.

9

Paolo Caliari known as Paolo Veronese
(Verona 1528–Venice 1588)
9. *Saint Francis Receiving the Stigmata*
10. *Saint Nicholas, Recognized as the Bishop of Myra*
Canvases, 256 × 432 cm, diam. 200 cm
Cats. 833, 661
Acquisition: 1919, *Saint Francis* returned from Austria; 1817, *Saint Nicholas* following the suppressions
Latest restoration: 1986

These paintings originally decorated both the ceiling of the demolished church of San Nicolò della Lattuga at the Frari, together with the *Adoration of the Magi* at the center and the four *Evangelists* at the corners (these five paintings are now on the ceiling of the chapel of the Rosary at the church of Santi Giovanni e Paolo). The *Saint Nicholas* painting was once rectangular, but like *Saint Francis,* was made circular to be set in the central space of the ceiling of the first room of the Galleries. The two canvases represent the artist's style in the 1580s, incorporating a darker palette in spite of the airy depths furrowed by light clouds, and significant attention to perspective. The paintings were completed near the reconsecration of the church, which took place in 1582.

10

Paolo Caliari known as Paolo Veronese, Workshop
(Verona 1528–Venice 1588)
11. *Assumption of the Virgin*
Canvas, 464 × 310 cm
Cat. 541
Acquisition: 1818–21, following the suppressions
Latest restoration: 1988

The large canvas decorated the ceiling of the refectory of the now demolished San Giacomo convent on Giudecca, flanked by two ovals with the *Annunciation* and the *Visitation* (in storage), and surrounded by a frieze with leaves, putti and figures. On the back wall was the *Feast in the House of Levi* (on deposit at the Verona City Hall), probably by Benedetto Caliari. Although this is a late work, and a collaboration— as is indicated by various sources—Paolo is surely responsible for much of the actual painting of the piece, and the scenic creation with the mannerist arbor, which has its origins in works by Correggio or Parmigianino.

11

12

13

Paolo Caliari known as Paolo Veronese
(Verona 1528–Venice 1588)
12. *Coronation of the Virgin*
Canvas, 405 × 219 cm
Cat. 264
Acquisition: 1812,
following the suppressions
Latest restoration: 1969

Originally the altarpiece
of the high altar of the church
of Ognissanti in Venice which
was consecrated on July 21,
1586, the date which should
also correspond to when the
painting was completed.
One of the artist's later works
(elaborated on a sketch
preserved at the Christ Church
in Oxford), which critics
have recently held to be
almost entirely the work
of the Veronese himself.
The coronation of Mary
is not a part of the evangelical
tradition, but was a very
diffuse devotional element at
the popular level. The Virgin
is crowned by the Holy Trinity
in the presence of angelic
choirs, the Evangelists,
Apostles and all the saints,
to whom the church was
of course dedicated
("Ognissanti," "All Saints").

Paolo Caliari known as Paolo Veronese
(Verona 1528–Venice 1588)
13. *Penitent San Jerome*
Canvas, 253 × 168 cm
Acquisition: Sant'Andrea
della Zirada
Latest restoration: 1988

Stored at the church of
Sant'Andrea della Zirada,
which was closed in 1971.
Originally it was to the right
of the high altar. This
painting also belongs to the
mature phase of the artist's
work, as revealed by the
beautifully rendered nude
and the quality of the wide
landscape to the right
of the saint's home, identified
with the usual attributes:
the domesticated lion, the
crucifix, the skull, the books,
the cardinal's hat hung on
the trunk. Dating to the end
of the 1570s, this is the
latest example of a theme
treated by Paolo in 1566 for
the church of Santa Maria
degli Angeli on Murano
(now at San Pietro Martire),
and on a painting at the
National Gallery in
Washington.

Room 6

7/8 Lorenzo Lotto, Savoldo, Romanino and Jacopo Palma il Vecchio

Along with Room 6, these two rooms
and the following, now used as a bookshop,
are part of the "Nuovissima" (very new)
wing of the Galleries that was constructed
between 1845 and 1875.
The rooms were remodeled by Carlo Scarpa
in 1949. Prior to this, in 1933, Room 7
was lined in green velvet and had been
reserved for two works by Giorgione:
the famous *Tempest*, and the *Nude*.
Scarpa added some false walls to the room,
thus creating a slightly trapezoid layout.

Lorenzo Lotto
*Portrait of a Gentleman
in His Study*, detail.

1

2

3

Giovanni Busi known as Cariani
(Venice 1485/90–
still living in 1547)
1. *Portrait of a Man*
Canvas, 68 × 56 cm
Cat. 299
Acquisition: 1850, from the
bequest of Felicita Renier
Latest restoration: 2005

Completed around 1517,
this portrait recalls the
Giorgione-influenced culture
in its use of color, and
in the expression and pose
of the subject.

Antonio Badile
(Verona 1518–1560)
2. *Portrait of Friar Salvo
Avanzi as Saint Thomas
Aquinas*
Canvas, 65 × 57 cm
Cat. 1318
Acquisition: 1957, by
purchase option
Latest restoration: 1958

This portrait, influenced
by Lotto, is signed and dated
on the back "M.D.XXX.XVI."
It depicts Avanzi with the
attitude and symbols
of Saint Thomas Aquinas,
whose Dominican order
the friar belonged to.

Giovanni Girolamo Savoldo
(Orzinuovi? 1480–ca. 1550)
3. *Saints Anthony Abbot
and Paul the Hermit*
Panel, 165 × 137 cm
Cat. 328
Acquisition: 1856, purchase
from the Manfrin collection
Latest restoration: 1977

On the stone at the bottom
is the signature and date,
perhaps decipherable as
1520. It is the first dated
work of the painter, who
appears to have been aware
of the innovations of the
Tuscan painters and the texts
of Dürer and Leonardo da
Vinci, but where a Lombard
element is particularly
noticeable.

**Alessandro Bonvicino
known as Moretto**
(Brescia 1498–1554)
4. *Saint Peter* and *Saint John
the Baptist*
Panels, 114 × 51 cm each
Cats. 332, 331
Acquisition: 1856, by
purchase from the Manfrin
collection
Latest restoration: 2005

Works originally part
of a polyptych that has
been dismembered. The
lost central panel may have
represented the Virgin and
Child. The cold, silvery color
harmonies, notably in the

figure of John the Baptist,
testify to the artist's
Lombard origins enriched
by his Venetian experience.
Datable to the early 1530s.

Bernardino Licinio
(Poscante ca. 1490–
Venice ca. 1565)
5. *Portrait of a Lady*
Canvas, 68 × 60 cm
Cat. 303
Acquisition: 1850, from
the bequest of Felicita Renier

At the base, the two coats
of arms with lions holding up
the sun and the moon belong
perhaps to the Morello
family of Treviso. From the
1540s, the portrait appears
to imitate Paris Bordon's
studies in color and form.

Bernardino Licinio
(Poscante ca. 1490–
Venice ca. 1565)
6. *Portrait of a Lady
with Balzo*
Canvas, 47 × 45 cm
Cat. 305
Acquisition: 1838,
by donation from
Girolamo Contarini

A fine example
of sixteenth-century
portraiture, this work
is characterized
by a warm tonality
and studied psychological
introspection.
Recently it has also
been attributed
to Palma il Vecchio.

4

5

6

Lorenzo Lotto
(Venice ca. 1480–Loreto 1556)
*7. Portrait of a Gentleman
in His Study*
Canvas, 97 × 110 cm
Cat. 912
Acquisition: 1930, by purchase
Latest restoration: 1997

Painted between 1528 and
1530, this is one of the most
famous portraits by Lotto.
The young melancholic man
is captured as a thought
distracts him from his
reading; his pallid face
emerging from the darkness
reveals a psychological
intensity that foreshadows
modern portraiture.
On the table, the rose
petals, ring, letters and small
lizard probably allude to the
transience of life, and perhaps
to an unhappy and lost love.

**Jacopo Negretti known as
Palma il Vecchio**
(Serina near Bergamo
1480–Venice 1528)
8. Assumption of the Virgin
Panel, 192 × 137 cm
Cat. 315
Acquisition: 1812,
following the suppressions
Latest restoration: 1993

From the Scuola di Santa
Maria Maggiore. The
painter received 50 ducats
on February 5, 1513, for
this piece. Two episodes
are depicted on it: the
Assumption of the Virgin and
the legend of the waistband
that she will give to Thomas
as proof of her rise to heaven.
The Mary we see here is not
extended upwards, but rather
turned in a human gesture
towards the small figure
of the Apostle coming
towards the mount to
witness the event.

**Jacopo Negretti known as
Palma il Vecchio
and Tiziano Vecellio
known as Titian**
(Serina near Bergamo
1480–Venice 1528;
Pieve di Cadore
ca. 1488/90–Venice 1576)

*9. Madonna and Child
with Saint Joseph between
Saints John the Baptist
and Catherine of Alexandria*

Canvas, 126 × 195 cm
Cat. 147
Acquisition: 1900, by
purchase
Latest restoration: 2000

7

8

78

9

One of Palma's masterpieces, which remained unfinished at his death but was brought to completion by Titian, who painted the head of the saint and the landscape with the castle and pillar behind the Virgin, as analysis under infrared and ultraviolet light has shown.

Tiziano Vecellio known as Titian, attr.
(Pieve di Cadore
ca. 1488/90–Venice 1576)
10. *Archangel Raphael and Tobias*
Panel, 170 × 149 cm
Cat. 1325
Acquisition: 1812,
following the suppressions
Latest restoration: 1994

From the church of Santa Caterina. Below at the center is the Bembo coat of arms. Cleaning has brought to light the outstanding quality of the work, leading recent critics to suggest that it was painted by Titian.

10

11

12

**Bonifacio de' Pitati
known as
Bonifacio Veronese**
(Verona 1487–Venice 1553)
11. *The Eternal Father
and Piazza San Marco*
Canvas, 165 × 130 cm
Cat. 917
Acquisition: 1919
Latest restoration: 1991

Originally the piece was the
central part of a triptych, with
the *Angels of the Annunciation*
at the sides and the *Virgin
Annunciate* (on display in the
Quadreria) from the Palazzo
Camerlenghi at Rialto. The
presence of the Loggetta of the
campanile—completed by
Sansovino in 1540—provides
a *post quem* date for the work,
being around 1543–44.
The view of San Marco reveals
certain details of a slice
of Venetian life:

in the foreground to the left
a furrier's shop, near the
campanile a group of acrobats,
and in front the porters.

**Bonifacio de' Pitati
known as
Bonifacio Veronese**
(Verona 1487–Venice 1553)
12. *Madonna and Child
Enthroned with Saint
Giovannino between Saints
Hombonus and Barbara
(Madonna of the Tailors)*
Canvas, 129 × 149 cm
Cat. 1305
Acquisition: 1945, from
Palazzo Reale

Signed and dated 1533, the
work was originally on the
altar of the Scuola dei Sartori
(Tailors' School), with its
symbol of a large scissors,
here depicted at the feet
of the Virgin. To the left,

Homobonus, the patron saint
of the tailors, gives alms to
a cripple: it is a clear message
of charity to the more wealthy
members of the Scuola.

Giorgio Vasari
(Arezzo 1511–Florence 1574)
13. *Justice*
14. *Putto with Plaque*
15. *Putto with Plaque*
16. *Patience*
Panels, 77 × 185 cm, 77 × 65
cm, 77 × 65 cm, 77 × 182 cm
Cats. 1370, 1372, 1373, 1371
Acquisition: 1987, by purchase
Latest restoration: 1989–90

These paintings come from
the ceiling of the Palazzo
Corner Spinelli on the
Grand Canal. The decoration
was completed in 1542
and included nine paintings
(such as the allegorical
figures of Faith, Hope and

Charity); the first two are
now in private collections
in London, while the third,
which ended up in Brera,
and later in the Museo
della Società di Studi Patri
Gallaratese (Gallarate,
Varese), was placed on
deposit at the Galleries
in 2002. The putti with
plaques are inspired by
high-reliefs presently at the
Archaeological Museum, but
which were once on the walls
of a building near Piazza
San Marco. The figures are
cut projecting out from an
invisible parapet against the
depths of Heaven, perfecting
an idea of Pordenone on the
lost ceiling of the Scuola di
San Francesco at the Frari.
This work attracted
considerable attention from
Venetian artists, particularly
Paolo Veronese.

13

14

17

Rocco Marconi
(Treviso ca. 1470/75–
recorded in Venice
from 1504, died before
May 13, 1529)
17. *Christ and the Adulteress*
Canvas, 131 × 197 cm
Cat. 1036
Acquisition: 1947, from
Palazzo Reale
Latest restoration: 1965

The painting, signed
"ROCHVS MARCHONIVS"
on the column beside Christ,
comes from the Venetian
monastery of San Giorgio
Maggiore. It represents a
subject that was very popular
in the artist's work. His
style reflects the fashion
for Orientalism which
spread to Venice in the

earlier sixteenth century.
The refined elegance
of the Magdalene indicates
the influence of the painting
of Palma il Vecchio, while
the grotesque heads
of some of the figures
are taken from Dürer.

15

16

18

19

Andrea Previtali
(Barbenno, Bergamo
1470/80–Bergamo 1528)
18. *Nativity*
19. *Crucifixion*
Canvases, 132 × 215 cm each
Cats. 639, 640
Acquisition: 1897, by
exchange from the
church of the Redentore
Latest restoration: 1982

Dating to between 1515 and
1520, these early paintings
were perhaps originally
in the Doge's Palace. The
admiration for Giovanni
Bellini and Lorenzo Lotto
is evident.

**Girolamo Romani known as
Romanino**
(Brescia 1484/87–ca. 1560)
20. *Lamentation Over the
Dead Christ and Donor*
Panel, 183 × 185 cm
Cat. 737
Acquisition: 1909,
by purchase
Latest restoration: 1975

An early work, signed
and dated 1510, originally
in the church of San Lorenzo
in Brescia. In addition
to the important elements
taken from Bellini, Giorgione
and Titian, there are also
significant Lombard
components, which in their
entirety form a balanced
synthesis of form and color.

**Sebastiano Luciani known as
Sebastiano del Piombo, attr.**
(Venice 1485–Rome 1547)
21. *Visitation*
Canvas, 209 × 150 cm
Cat. 95
Acquisition: 1814,
following the suppressions
Latest restoration: 2004

Formerly in the monastery
of Sant'Andrea, the work
has been variously
attributed to the great
Venetian Cinquecento
masters: the young Titian,
Sebastiano del Piombo
and Giovanni Cariani.
The present restoration,
while revealing the poor
state of preservation due to
cleaning at some early date,
has bolstered the attribution
to Sebastiano del Piombo
and revealed the work's
close ties to the *Sacred
Conversations* in the
Louvre and the Metropolitan
Museum, New York.

20

21

10 Titian, Jacopo Tintoretto and Paolo Veronese

Begun by Francesco Lazzari in 1828, the room was inaugurated in 1834. The passage between this room and its twin hall (Room 11) is decorated with four columns in Greek marble from the Scuola di Santa Maria della Misericordia.

Titian
Pietà, detail.

1

2

3

**Paolo Caliari known as
Paolo Veronese**
(Verona 1528–Venice 1588)
1. *Virgin and Child
Enthroned with Saints
Joseph, Justina, Francis,
Young John the Baptist
and Jerome*
Canvas, 338 × 187 cm
Cat. 37
Acquisition: 1817,
following the suppressions
Latest restoration: 1969–70

Originally on the altar
of the sacristy of the church
of San Zaccaria, the work
was taken to Paris in 1797
and then returned and given
to the Accademia in 1815
in exchange for three
paintings which are still in
the church. In 1562 Francesco
Bonaldo undertook to pay
200 ducats to refit the sacristy
and the altarpiece should date
to slightly later, around 1564.
The artist appears particularly
interested in the relationship
with the environment where
the painting was originally
kept, an aspect which
is of course now lost. The
mannerist elements present
here work harmoniously
and with an almost classical
sense of balance, evidence
that Veronese had taken
in the great devotional
tradition of the fifteenth and
sixteenth centuries explored
by artists from Giovanni
Bellini to Titian.

**Paolo Caliari known as
Paolo Veronese**
(Verona 1528–Venice 1588)
2. *Feast in the House of Levi*
Canvas, 560 × 1309 cm
Cat. 203
Acquisition: 1815,
following the suppressions
Latest restoration: 1980–82

This great painting, which
was taken to Paris and then
returned in 1815, was
originally a *Last Supper* for
the refectory of the convent
of Santi Giovanni e Paolo,
as a replacement for a *Last
Supper* by Titian that had
been lost in a fire. According
to the writing at the base
of the pillar bottom left,
the work was completed
on April 20, 1573, but
three months later the artist
was accused of heresy
for this vast composition
which contained what were
considered to be excessive

anti-conformist elements.
In spite of his strong
defence of his artistic
freedom, Veronese was
ordered to "correct" the
painting at his own expense
within three months.
But the only change he
made was to add the writing
on the top of the pillar
with the date below, clearly
at the suggestion of
Dominican scholars:
"fecit D. Covi Magnum
Levi—Luca Cap. V," so as
to avoid a scandal. In fact,
Luke says in chapter V
of his Gospel: "Levi held a
great banquet for the Lord."
In the work, with its triple-
arch background inspired
by the buildings of Palladio
and Sansovino, Veronese's
research into the idea of the
banquet is concluded, with
the attainment of a complete
balance of scenic elements
and figures.

**Paolo Caliari known as
Paolo Veronese**
(Verona 1528–Venice 1588)
3. *Allegory of the Battle
of Lepanto*
Canvas, 170 × 137 cm
Cat. 212
Acquisition: 1812,
following the suppressions
Latest restoration: 1983

Originally in the church
of San Pietro Martire on
Murano, to the right of the
Rosary altar, while to the left
was the *Madonna of the
Rosary*, dated 1573
(Quadreria, cat. 207),
completed by the workshop
based on a Veronese
drawing. In the lower area
is depicted the Battle of
Lepanto of 1571, which
was between the Lega Santa
and the Turkish Fleet, also
commemorated by prints
at around that time.
On the upper part is Venice

between Saint Mark and
Saint Justina, on whose feast
day the battle took place.
Venice is shown being
presented to the Virgin,
while to the left Saint Peter
and Saint Roch intercede
for her. The small canvas,
clearly by the artist himself,
was perhaps commissioned
in 1573 as an ex voto by
Pietro Giustinian of Murano,
who had distinguished
himself in the battle, or
by Onfrè Giustinian who
brought news of the victory
to Venice.

Room 10

4

Jacopo Robusti known as Jacopo Tintoretto
(Venice 1519–1594)
4. *Transport of the Body of Saint Mark*
Canvas, 397 × 315 cm
Cat. 831
Acquisition: 1920, from the Salone Sansoviniano of the Libreria Marciana
Latest restoration: 1991–92

Painted between 1562 and 1566 for the Scuola Grande di San Marco (where the three paintings following

works are also from, while a final one with the *Discovery of the Body of Saint Mark* is in the Brera Gallery in Milan), paid for by the Guardian Grande Tommaso Rangone. The work attests to Tintoretto's exceptionally imaginative and evocative style, and reveals the new luminism which typifies Tintoretto's paintings from this period.

Jacopo Robusti known as Jacopo Tintoretto
(Venice 1519–1594)
5. *Miracle of Saint Mark Freeing the Slave*
Canvas, 416 × 544 cm
Cat. 42
Acquisition: 1821, with the works returned to Venice from Paris
Latest restoration: 1965

This was the first painting made by Tintoretto for the Chapter Hall of the Scuola Grande di San Marco.

Brought to Paris in 1797, it was returned in 1815 and entrusted to the Accademia Galleries. It was probably commissioned in 1547 and completed by April of 1548, when Aretino praised the work in a letter to Tintoretto. The scene is of a condemned slave being freed as a result of the intercession of Saint Mark. The slave was to be blinded and have his legs broken because—against the wishes of his master—he had gone to worship the relics of the saint. In this work, with its remarkable new dramatic effect and intense use of color, the various figurative phases of the artist are summarized, especially the Michelangelo-influenced aspects, rendered through a methodical graphic effort, in a vision of such newness that it could only provoke wonder and bewilderment from his contemporaries.

Jacopo Robusti known as Jacopo Tintoretto
(Venice 1519–1594)
6. *Rescue at Sea*
Canvas, 396 × 334 cm
Cat. 832
Acquisition: 1920, from the Salone Sansoviniano of the Libreria Marciana
Latest restoration: 1992–93

Painted between 1562 and 1566, this painting depicts the miraculous rescue of a Saracen sailor who at the turn of Alexandria had called upon the saint during a storm. The painting is composed of two pieces which reveal transparent pencil sketches on the back, with no relation to the final composition but which indicate how Tintoretto used different fragments of canvas. This work is especially fascinating for its dramatic rendering

5

of the turbulent seas and the extremely adept use of contrasts in light.

Jacopo Robusti known as Jacopo Tintoretto Domenico Robusti known as Domenico Tintoretto
(Venice 1519–1594;
(Venice 1560–1635)
7. *The Dream of Saint Mark*
Canvas, 388 × 314 cm
Cat. 875

Acquisition: 1924, from the church of Santa Maria degli Angeli at Murano
Latest restoration: 1992–93

A collaborative effort by Jacopo Tintoretto and his son Domenico, originally located at the side of the altar in the chapel of the Chapter Room of the Scuola Grande di San Marco, which Jacopo strove to complete in 1585

in order for his son, son-in-law and two friends to gain acceptance into the Dominican confraternity. The invention of the angel who appears before the sleeping Mark, was doubtless the work of Domenico.

6

7

8

9

Jacopo Robusti known as Jacopo Tintoretto
(Venice 1519–1594)
8. *Virgin and Child between Saints Cecilia, Marina, Theodore, Cosma and Damian*
Canvas, 341 × 251 cm
Cat. 221
Acquisition: 1812, following the suppressions
Latest restoration: 1991–92

This piece was originally on the first altar on the left in the church of Santi Cosma e Damiano on the island of Giudecca. It dates to the 1550s, as confirmed by the most recent restoration. The chromatic alternation of the once much lighter large clouds is unfortunately irreversible.

Paolo Caliari known as Paolo Veronese
(Verona 1528–Venice 1588)
9. *Mystic Marriage of Saint Catherine*
Canvas, 377 × 241 cm
Cat. 1324
Acquisition: 1918, taken back after the First World War from the church of Santa Caterina, became State property following the suppressions
Latest restoration: 1986

Painted for the high altar of the Venetian church of Santa Caterina. The painting was taken from the church during the World War I. The emphasis is by now pre-Baroque, with its marvelous chromatic elements and serene beauty of the images. The piece was very well received by contemporaries and artists of the following century. Dated around 1575, near the time when Veronese painted the canvases for the ceiling of the Sala del Collegio in the Doge's Palace.

10

Tiziano Vecellio known as Titian
(Pieve di Cadore
ca. 1488/90–Venice 1576)
10. *Pietà*
Canvas, 353 × 347 cm
Cat. 400
Acquisition: 1814,
following the suppressions
Latest restoration: 2007

This work reached the
Accademia from the church
of Sant'Angelo, where it had
been placed in 1631 at the
end of the great plague.
Ridolfi, in 1648, recalls
how it had been created

by Titian for the chapel
of Christ at the Frari in
exchange for his being buried
there. But the negotiations
failed and the painting,
created from seven different
pieces of canvas, was brought
into the workshop. A
document discovered in the
secret Archive of the Vatican
confirms that in March of
1575 the painting was
displayed at the Frari. In fact,
a papal nuncio decree asks
that the image, which was
placed on a different altar
from the one agreed upon, be
returned to Titian. In 1576,

while the plague was at its
worst, Titian had nearly
transformed the work into
a large ex voto against the
epidemic, an exceptional
autobiographical statement.
As the writing near the
bottom attests, it was
finished by Jacopo Palma il
Giovane after Titian's death
on August 27 of that year:
"quod Titianus inchoatum
reliquit, Palma reventer
absolvit deoq dicavit opus"
("that which Titian left
unfinished, Palma brought
reverently to completion and
dedicated the work to God").

Palma's actual interventions
were primarily some touches
to camouflage the various
grafts of canvas, the angel
with the torch painted over a
previous putto left unfinished
by Titian, and the writing
itself. The work is centered
largely around the theme
of death, eucharistic
sacrifice and resurrection.
Like Michelangelo, Titian
also portrayed himself
in the *Pietà* destined for
his grave: the old man lying
prostrate in front of the
Virgin—probably Saint
Jerome—is a self-portrait.

11

Paolo Caliari known as Paolo Veronese
(Verona 1528–Venice 1588)
11. *Annunciation*
Canvas, 271 × 541 cm
Cat. 260
Acquisition: 1812,
following the suppressions
Latest restoration: 2007

From the Scuola dei Mercanti (still intact at the left of the church of Madonna dell'Orto), where the piece was kept in the Sala dell'Albergo above the door. The symbol of the confraternity—a hand blessing the cross—can be seen at the center under the drum, while on the pillars of the middle columns are the coats of arms of the commissioners, the Cadabrazzo and Cottoni families. The work was widely praised by contemporaries. It was painted in 1578, a date revealed by reflection analysis under a thick repainted layer which, together with other alterations (the insertion of a piece of floor on the lower central area near the door), greatly influence our understanding of the piece. The composition appears as a succession and synthesis of scenic elements, closed at the background by a small temple which was perhaps inspired by the church of Santa Maria Nuova in Vicenza, completed by Palladio also in 1578. The preparatory drawing was in charcoal for the architectural structure with brushstrokes added freehand in the figures. Especially well preserved are the angel and some remarkable details such as the vase on the balustrade, where the painting retains all its original brightness.

12

**Paolo Caliari known as
Paolo Veronese**
(Verona 1528–Venice 1588)
12. *Crucifixion*
Canvas, 285 × 447 cm
Cat. 255
Acquisition: 1834,
following the suppressions
Latest restoration: 1969

The freedom of the *Feast
in the House of Levi* is
replaced here by a strict
adhesion to the evangelical
text, a sign of a deep change
in the political and religious
climate in Venice, surely
accelerated by the plague

of 1575. The dark and
dramatic atmosphere
of the scenes is typical
of Veronese's last phase,
to which the painting
belongs; it was completed
around 1582 and was
originally in the church
of San Nicolò della Lattuga
at the Frari.

11 Leandro Bassano, Bernardo Strozzi, Giambattista Tiepolo, Luca Giordano, Jacopo Tintoretto, Bonifacio Veronese and Pordenone

Room 11 was reopened in 1946
by Carlo Scarpa after covering it
with a thick grey canvas. This was to be
a provisional arrangement while a definitive
plan was implemented—which was not
to be carried out by Scarpa. In the 1980s,
this large room was renovated, repeating the
motives he used in its twin room (Room 10).
In 1996, fragments of the ceiling
from the church of the Scalzi painted
by Giambattista Tiepolo were placed
here, using specially created supports
for their display.

Giambattista Tiepolo
*The Discovery of the True Cross
and Saint Helena*, detail.

94

Leandro da Ponte known as Leandro Bassano
(Bassano 1557–1622)
1. *Resurrection of Lazarus*
Canvas, 416 × 237 cm
Cat. 252
Acquisition: 1815,
following the suppressions
Latest restoration: 1981

This altarpiece, originally
on the altar of the Mocenigo
house in the church of Santa
Maria della Carità, was
taken to Paris and later
returned in 1815.
Generally believed
to be from the beginning
of the seventeenth century,
the painting reveals
Bassano's dignified
translation of his father
Jacopo's artistic language.

Bernardo Strozzi
(Genoa 1581–Venice 1644)
2. *Portrait of the Knight
Giovanni Grimani*
Canvas, 225 × 143 cm
Cat. 1358
Acquisition: 1981,
by purchase
Latest restoration: 1995

Giovanni Grimani, while he
was ambassador in Vienna
from 1636 to 1640, was
knighted by the Emperor.
This large portrait was
probably ordered from Strozzi
upon his return from Vienna,
immediately after 1640.
Grimani is portrayed with
the golden stole, symbol
of knighthood. This work is
a masterpiece from the height
of Strozzi's artistic maturity.
Hints of Rubens and Van
Dyck are brought together
with a decidedly Venetian
treatment of light and color.
The great painters of the
eighteenth century, from
Fra' Galgario to Alessandro
Longhi and including
Giambattista Tiepolo
himself, will look to this
kind of portraiture for their
official portraits.

1

3

Bernardo Strozzi
(Genoa 1581–Venice 1644)
3. *Feast in the House of Simon*
Canvas, 257 × 737 cm
Cat. 777
Acquisition: 1911,
by purchase
Latest restoration: 1981

This large painting,
purchased in Vicenza in 1911,
comes from the chapel
of Palazzo Gorleri in Genoa.
It was probably originally
painted for the parlor
of the Santa Maria in
Passione monastery
in Genoa. In addition to its
attempt to translate the style
of Caravaggio into a Baroque
setting, the painting reveals
a distinct Venetian influence,
a style well known to Strozzi
even before he moved
to Venice.

2

4

Giambattista Tiepolo
(Venice 1696-Madrid 1770)
4. *Punishment*
of the Serpents
Canvas, 167 × 1355 cm
Cat. 343
Acquisition: 1892,
following the suppressions
Latest restoration: 1992

This large frieze was
originally under the choir
in the church of Santi Cosma
e Damiano on the Giudecca

(Zanetti 1771). It was
owned by the State after
the suppressions, and ended
up in the church of Santa
Maria e San Liberale
in Castelfranco Veneto,
where it remained rolled-up
for almost sixty years.
These events damaged the
work, but all its expressive
potential remains intact;
indeed, it is precisely for this
reason that the large gaps
have not been filled in.

Dating to around 1731–32,
the painting depicts the
biblical episode of the bronze
serpent erected by Moses in
the desert in order to heal
the wounds of snakes sent
by God to punish the people
of Israel who had not shown
the proper faith or patience.

**Giambattista Tiepolo
and Girolamo Mengozzi
known as Colonna**
(Venice 1696–Madrid 1770;

(Ferrara ca. 1688–
Venice 1744)
5. *Moses and Aaron*
6. *Announcement*
to the Prophet Nathan
7. *David and His Wife Mikal*
Removed frescoes,
335 × 446 × 180 cm each
Cats. 1376, 1378, 1377
Latest restoration: 1995–96

The Scalzi Carmelites
commissioned Tiepolo
to decorate the ceiling

5

6

of the church of Santa Maria di Nazareth, the last of the great religious cycles on fresco by the artist. The church was destroyed by an Austrian bomb intended for the nearby railway station on the night of October 24, 1915. The contract was stipulated on September 13, 1743, and on October 1 Girolamo Mengozzi, nicknamed "Colonna" (column), began to create the artificial architectural features

for the sum of 1500 ducats; Tiepolo would receive 3,000 ducats for his work. He studied the composition in a considerable number of sketches and prepared two oval drafts on canvas: the first, probably the one for which he was paid 100 *zecchini* on September 13, 1743, is now preserved in the Accademia Gallery (Room 16, cat. 911); the second, which was closest to the final version, is today

at the Paul Getty Museum in Malibu. Payments were made from April 14 until November 23, 1745, dates which should also correspond to the actual execution of the vast work. On the central part was celebrated the miraculous *Transportation of the Holy House of Nazareth*. In the decoration on the perimeter of the vault were other episodes depicting various parts of the Old Testament

foreshadowing Mary herself, or the theme of the Holy House. Another four pendentives, one of which is lost, depicted Annunciation scenes. Recovered from the depository where they had been stored after the disaster, they were then transferred onto canvas in 1969. The last part of the work restored the slightly curved shape. On the first, a few condensed episodes from Exodus are represented: Moses, angered by the smelting of the golden calf, breaks the tablets of the law bestowed upon him by God, which will be given to him a second time. Returning from Mount Sinai, his face becomes radiant after having spoken with the Lord and thus he appears to Aaron. On the second, God, in the form of an angel, announces to the prophet Nathan his alliance with David and the permanence of his dynasty, the depository of the messianic promises. On the last one, David responds harshly to his wife Mikal, who had chastised him for humiliating himself by dancing before the ark of the Lord. The impressive power of the line, the suggestion of the green tones on the light background and the effective synthesis make these fragments—which are clearly by the artist himself, at least the figurative parts— works of the utmost quality. As documentation also confirms, the backgrounds belong to Mengozzi, while Tiepolo had to unify the whole work with small retouches. His unmistakable luminous brushstrokes are found in many areas on these three pendentives and on the following four loggias.

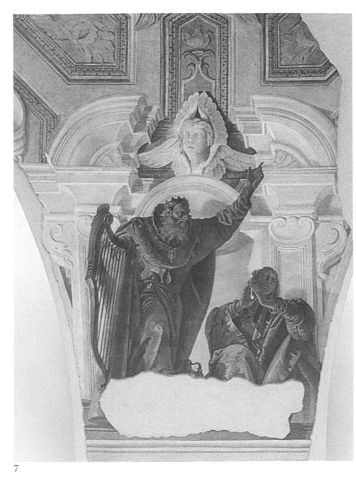

7

Room 11

8

9

10

11

12

**Giambattista Tiepolo
and Girolamo Mengozzi
known as Colonna**
(Venice 1696–Madrid 1770;
(Ferrara ca. 1688–Venice
1744)
8. *Worshippers Facing
a Loggia*
9. *Loggia*
10. *Worshippers Facing
a Loggia*
11. *Worshippers Facing
a Loggia*
Removed frescoes,
405 × 216 cm each
Cats. 836, 1375, 837, 1374
Latest restoration: 1995–96

At the four curved corners
of the ceiling of the Santa
Maria di Nazareth were
some railed galleries which
survived the Austrian
bombing of 1915 and were

recovered between 1916
and 1917. Two of these
(cats. 836, 837) were
displayed at the Accademia
Galleries in 1919, the other
two remained in storage until
the most recent restoration.
On three of these, Tiepolo
painted some praying
worshippers, awed spectators
of the miracle.
The fourth, which is
empty, should belong to
Girolamo Mengozzi, known
as Colonna, but here as
in the other loggias, Tiepolo
surely intervened with
some corrections in order
to render the work more
uniform.

Giambattista Tiepolo
(Venice 1696–Madrid 1770)
12. *The Discovery of the True
Cross and Saint Helena*
Canvas, diameter 500 cm
Cat. 462
Acquisition: 1812,
following the suppressions
Latest restoration: 1982

The large ceiling painting
was made for the church
of the Cappuccine in
Castello, which was
destroyed.
The painting was
surrounded by decorations
by Girolamo Mengozzi
(Colonna). From about
the same time as the first
works delivered in 1743
by Tiepolo to the Scuola
dei Carmini, it shares
with these the marvelous

chromatic polyphony
and refined "upside-down"
perspective. A sketch
showing an early idea
for the painting is also
on display in the Galleries
(Room 16, cat. 789).

13

Luca Giordano
(Naples 1634–1705)
13. *Crucifixion of Saint Peter*
Canvas, 195 × 257 cm
Cat. 751
Acquisition: 1910,
by purchase
Latest restoration: 1984

The signature and the
date are on the painting:
"L. Giordano F. 1692," but
these have been recognized
as false. The authorship is
certain, but the date is less
so, with critics generally
placing the work—still with
some exceptions—around
1659–60. The dramatic
component of the
composition evokes the
paintings of Caravaggio,
but the diluition of the forms
into the colors prefigures
a Rococo style.

14

15

Jacopo Robusti known as Jacopo Tintoretto
(Venice 1519–1594)
14. *Madonna and Child Enthroned with Saints Sebastian, Mark, Theodore and Treasurers* (*Madonna of the Treasurers*)
Canvas, 221 × 520 cm
Cat. 210
Acquisition: 1883
Latest restoration: 1992

This large painting, also known as the *Madonna of the Treasurers*, carries the inscription on the lower left: "unanimis concordiae / simbolus / 1566."
The work was destined for the Palazzo dei Camerlenghi at Rialto. The Camerlenghi were the financial magistrates of the Venetian Republic. The date of 1566 refers to the offices of Michele Pisani, Lorenzo Dolfin and Marino Malipiero, whose coats of arms are shown on the plinth to the lower left, but the actual execution of the piece occurred when Marino Malipiero's command ended in around 1567, a date which can actually be seen under magnification just below that of "1566." The horizontal development of the composition, emphasized by the succession of porticoes with the marvelous landscape beyond them, and the penetrating characterization of the commissioners followed by their secretaries make this work a masterpiece of the Venetian votive painting tradition.

Jacopo Robusti known as Jacopo Tintoretto
(Venice 1519–1594)
15. *Crucifixion*
Canvas, 280 × 444 cm
Cat. 213
Acquisition: 1891, from the Scuola del Rosario in the church of Santi Giovanni e Paolo
Latest restoration: 1967

Originally in the Scuola del Santissimo Sacramento, in the Venetian church of San Severo, this piece dates to around 1554–55 and reveals a period in which Tintoretto embraced the painting of Paolo Veronese.

Room 11

16

Bonifacio de' Pitati known as Bonifacio Veronese
(Verona 1487–Venice 1553)
16. *Lazarus the Beggar*
Canvas, 206 × 438 cm
Cat. 291
Acquisition: 1812, by purchase
Latest restoration: 1991–92

Purchased from the Grimani family for the Accademia Galleries at the request of the viceroy Eugenio Beauharnais; originally the piece was in the Palazzo Giustiniani, where it was still recorded in 1763. The episode depicted here refers to the evangelical parable of Epulone refusing to give alms to poor Lazarus,

but here this becomes the pretext for an exceptional description of Venetian villa life. Dated around 1543–45, this is considered the artist's masterpiece for his ability to bring together the teaching of both Titian and Tintoretto.

Giovanni Antonio de' Sacchis known as Pordenone
(Pordenone 1483/84–Ferrara 1539)
17. *The Blessed Lorenzo Giustiniani and Saints*
Canvas, 420 × 222 cm
Cat. 316
Acquisition: 1815, following the suppressions
Latest restoration: 1997

This altarpiece was commissioned from Pordenone in 1532 for 100 ducats, and was for the altar of the Renier family, which is still in the church of Madonna dell'Orto. Brought to Paris in 1797, it was returned to Venice in 1815 and entrusted

to the Accademia Galleries. The figure of Lorenzo Giustiniani—canonized in 1690—blesses Saints Louis of Toulouse, Francis, Bernard of Siena, John the Baptist and two "turchini," who were secular canons from San Giorgio in Alga, to which order the church was entrusted. The articulation of the composition, the elongated modes and twists of the figures, and in particular the pose of the Michelangelesque body of John the Baptist, are all characteristics of mannerism, which was effectively introduced in Veneto by Pordenone himself.

17

12   Marco Ricci, Giuseppe Zais and Francesco Zuccarelli

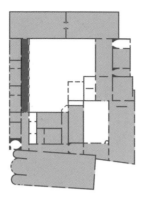

This room is formed by the long end
of the Palladio hallway, with its large windows
which are probably the work of Lazzari
in the nineteenth century. In 1912 three doors
and their awnings were installed; these
may have come from a palazzo in Brescia,
and were painted by Pietro Scalvini
(Brescia 1718–1792) and Saverio Gandini
(Cremona ca. 1729–Brescia 1796).

Francesco Zuccarelli
Landscape with a Lady
on Horseback, detail.

1

2

Marco Ricci
(Belluno 1676–Venice 1730)
1. *Landscape with a Stream, Monks and Washerwomen*
2. *Landscape with Horses at the Trough*
Canvases, 136 × 98 cm each
Cats. 457, 456
Acquisition: 1878,
by purchase
Latest restoration: 2008

The two pendants are recorded in the Corniani Algarotti gallery in Treviso. In the first the Piave valley is discernable, and it also seems to appear in the second, where an old fountain is also shown. They represent two works of fundamental importance in the output of the artist, who was inspired by the drawings of Titian and the engravings of Domenico Campagnola, as well as favoring lively, realistic observation. Dated in the past to 1720, more recent scholars have rightly brought forward the two landscapes to about 1715.

Giuseppe Zais, attr.
(Canale d'Agordo 1709–Treviso 1781)
3. *Landscape with Agar and the Angel*
4. *Landscape with Tobias and the Angel*
Canvases, 71 × 94 cm, 72 × 96 cm
Cats. 721, 722
Acquisition: 1906,
by purchase
Latest restoration: 1984

These paintings with the two biblical stories immersed in the landscape—as they also occur in Fetti's "Parables"— are traditionally attributed to Zais, although they seem closer to the style of Antonio Diziani.

3

4

5

6

7

Giuseppe Zais
(Canale d'Agordo 1709–
Treviso 1781)
5. *Ancient Ruins with
a Large Arch and Columns*
6. *Landscape with a Stream
and Dancing Villagers*
Canvases, 96 × 146 cm,
196 × 142 cm
Cats. 847, 848
Acquisition: 1923, from
the Palazzo Reale
Latest restoration: 1984

In these landscapes from
the end of the 1730s, the
influence of Marco Ricci
on Zais's work is quite clear;
Zais renders Ricci's style
more elegant, but keeps
it vivid and bright.

Francesco Zuccarelli
(Pitigliano 1702–
Florence 1788/89)
7. *The Rape of Europa*
Canvas, 143 × 208 cm
Cat. 858
Acquisition: 1923, from
the Palazzo Reale
Latest restoration: 1982

On the collar of the dog
at the lower left is the
signature. This canvas,
like its pendant with the

Bacchanal (Room 12,
cat. 859), was painted for
the Pisani family, who
had dedicated a wing of their
splendid and regal villa
in Stra to landscape painting.
It dates to around 1740–50
and is considered the artist's
masterpiece. The story
of the rape of Europa, taken
from Ovid's *Metamorphoses*,
is rendered with the
same grace and ease as
a Metastasian melodramma.

Room 12

Giuseppe Zais
(Canale d'Agordo 1709–
Treviso 1781)
8. *Landscape with a River,
Bridge and Flocks*
9. *Ruins of a Vaulted
Building*
Canvases, 97 × 142 cm,
97 × 147 cm
Cats. 849, 846
Acquisition: 1923,
from the Palazzo Reale
Latest restoration:
Landscape 1985; *Ruins* 1984

Marco Ricci's influence
on Zais is also evident
in these paintings from the
end of the 1730s. Zais renders
Ricci's style more elegant,
but keeps it vivid and bright.

8

Francesco Zuccarelli
(Pitigliano 1702–
Florence 1788/89)
10. *Landscape with a Lady
on Horseback*
11. *Landscape with a Boy
Fishing*
Canvas, transported from
another canvas, 115 × 133 cm;
canvas, 116 × 135 cm
Cats. 861, 862
Acquisition: 1923, from
the Palazzo Reale
Latest restoration:
Landscape with Lady 1984;
Landscape with Boy 1985

These two landscapes once
belonged to the Pisani family,
and date to around 1740–50.
They present with gentle
and festive grace and fresh
colors the pastoral theme
that was so dear to
eighteenth-century poetics.

9

10

11

12

Francesco Zuccarelli
(Pitigliano 1702–
Florence 1788/89)
12. *Bacchanal*
Canvas, 142 × 209 cm
Cat. 859
Acquisition: 1923, from
the Palazzo Reale
Latest restoration: 1982

Pendant of the *Rape of
Europa* (Room 12, cat. 858),
also belonging to the Pisani
family and painted during
the same period. While fauns
and nymphs dance together
in the idyllic landscape,
the drunk Bacchus rests
in the shade of a rustic hut.

Francesco Zuccarelli
(Pitigliano 1702–Florence
1788/89)
13. *Hunt for the Bull*
Canvas, 114 × 150 cm
Cat. 864
Acquisition: 1949, from
the Palazzo Reale
Latest restoration: 1984

Originally in the Benedictine
convent of San Giorgio
Maggiore, this work is
considered to be from
the early period of the artist's
career, a little after 1732,
when he arrived in Venice.

Even the bloody episode
here of the hunt for the bull
is interpreted with a pastoral
grace, and the work was
widely praised in artistic
centers such as Paris
and London, where the
artist sojourned.

13

14

15

16

17

Antonio Diziani
(Venice 1737–1797)
14. *Landscape
with Mary Magdalene*
Canvas, 132 × 117 cm
Cat. 455
Acquisition: 1807, from
the old Accademia

This is the painting that
Antonio Diziani—the son
of the more famous Gaspare—
presented in 1766 to gain
admittance to the Accademia,
into which he was accepted
only on September 11, 1774.

Gaspare Diziani
(Belluno 1689–Venice 1767)
15. *Moses and the Burning
Bush*
16. *Moses Receiving
the Tablets of the Law*
Canvases, 56 × 96 cm each
Cats. 459, 460
Acquisition: 1838,
following the suppressions
Latest restoration: 1980

These two pendants
are largely considered
to have been painted

in collaboration with the
artist's son Antonio, who
worked on the landscape.

Francesco Zuccarelli
(Pitigliano 1702–
Florence 1788/89)
17. *Landscape with a Resting
Hunter*
Canvas, 79 × 97 cm
Cat. 1333
Acquisition: 1959, from
the Palazzo Reale
Latest restoration: 1993

Originally perhaps in the
convent of San Giorgio
Maggiore, this painting—of
which there is a copy on the
antiquities market—dates
to around the 1740s.
The typical idyllic
representation of nature,
rendered with
an unusual naturalness,
is strong in the group
with the resting hunter,
the horse and the two dogs.
This aspect reveals
Zuccarelli's familiarity
with Dutch landscape
artists such as Berchem
and Wouwermann.

**Saverio Gandini
and Pietro Scalvini**
(Cremona ca. 1729–
Brescia 1796;
Brescia 1718–1798)
18. *Architectural View
with Allegory of Architecture*
(door panel)
19. *Landscape with Classical
Buildings* (transom panel)
20. *Architectural View
with Allegory of Painting*
(door panel)
21. *Landscape with Classical
Buildings* (door panel)
22. *Architectural View
with Allegory of Sculpture*
(door panel)
23. *Landscape with Classical
Buildings* (transom panel)
Door panels, 198 × 83 cm
each (figured part
109 × 57 cm)
Transom panels, 85 × 112 cm
each (figured part
75 × 104 cm)

Cats. 1441–1445, 1448
Acquisition: 1912,
by purchase
Latest restoration: 2000

The doors have mixtilinear
central panels, set
within carved gilt frames,
representing imaginary
architectural views,
with figures busy practicing
architecture, painting
and sculpture. Some
scenes contain the names
of the artists Gandini
and Scalvini and the
years 1778 and 1779.
Transom panels appear
above the doors, with views
of landscapes and ruins
of classical buildings.
They probably come
from an ancient palazzo
in Brescia and were
placed in the rooms
of the Palladian loggia.

18

19

20

21

22

23

13 Jacopo Bassano, Portraits by Jacopo Tintoretto, Giovanni Bellini, Andrea Mantegna, Piero della Francesca, Cosmè Tura, Hans Memling and Giorgione

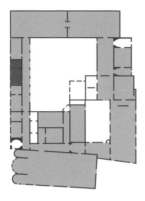

Obtained by the unification of three cells of the Carità convent, with the first remodeling projects. The ceiling of the first area, which had previously been under a large canvas, was recovered, revealing the decoration by Tranquillo Orsi. The remodeling was carried out by Carlo Scarpa in 1947.
In this room, temporarily displayed with a new installation, are the works from Rooms 4 and 5 (which are presently undergoing restoration).

Giovanni Bellini
*Madonna and Child
with Saint John the Baptist
and Saint*, detail.

1

2

Giovanni Bellini
(Venice 1434/39–1516)
1. *Virgin and Child*
Panel, 77 × 57 cm
Cat. 583
Acquisition: 1812,
following the suppressions
Latest restoration: 1938

Traditionally identified
as the *Madonna* which
was once in the Palazzo dei
Camerlenghi, the treasurers
of the Venetian State,
at the Rialto, although
there is no trace of the gold
ground which that piece
supposedly had.
The painting dates to the
1470s and already reveals
some of the typical traits
of many Bellini Madonnas,
where the influence of
Mantegna—the artist's

brother-in-law—is softened
by a new sense of spirituality
and humanity.

Andrea Mantegna
(Isola di Cartura, Padua
1431/32–Mantua 1506)
2. *Saint George*
Panel, 66 × 32 cm
Cat. 588
Acquisition: 1856, by
purchase from the Manfrin
collection
Latest restoration: 1992

Dated about 1446, this
painting is believed
to have been the side panel
of a polyptych, but no
confirmation of this has as
yet been found. The stern
young man—more mythical
hero than Christian saint—
wears a breast-plate
inspired by a drawing
of Jacopo Bellini, Mantegna's
father-in-law. The fortified
city in the background—also

taken from a drawing
by Jacopo—is a depiction
of Selene, where according
to the legend Saint George
slew the dragon.

3

4

Piero della Francesca
(Borgo San Sepolcro
1416/17–1492)
*3. Saint Jerome
and a Devotee*
Panel, 49 × 42 cm
Cat. 47
Acquisition: 1850, from the
bequest of Felicita Renier
Latest restoration: 2007
(maintenance)

The artist's signature
"Pietri de bu/go sci sep/ulcri
opus" (a work of Pietro di
Borgo San Sepolcro) can be
seen on the trunk of the tree
where the cross is mounted.
Although he has none
of the traditional attributes,
the devotee kneeling before
Saint Jerome was recognized
by a later inscription as
the Venetian Girolamo

Amadi di Agostino, originally
of Lucca. The work was
intended for private
devotion, and presents
a new, more balanced
rapport between saint and
worshipper, with the
devotee portrayed in natural
proportions. The landscape
shows the homeland
of the painter, San Sepolcro,
and the Tiber Valley
(although all the green
components have
unfortunately turned brown).
Probably an early work,
it can be dated to around
the 1450s.

Cosmè Tura
(Ferrara 1430–1495)
*4. Madonna and Child
(Madonna of the Zodiac)*
Panel, 61 × 41 cm
Cat. 628
Acquisition: 1896, by
purchase
Latest restoration: 1982

A work by the master of the
fifteenth century Ferrarese
School of painting, dated
to around the 1480s.
This painting was probably
conceived for a private
residence, as the inscription
near the bottom would
indicate: "Sviglia el tuo figlio
dolce madre pia / per far
infin felice l'alma mia"
("Wake your son, oh pious
sweet mother / and so
make joyful my soul").

On the spandrel of the frame,
two angels hold aloft the
symbol of Saint Bernard,
while the bunches of grapes
with the goldfinch and
the wallcreeper are symbols
of the Passion and
Resurrection of Christ.
The small panel is also called
the *Madonna of the Zodiac*,
for the zodiacal signs traced
in gold on the background;
the signs for Acquarius,
Pisces, Sagittarius and Virgo
are still legible, while those
to the right have all nearly
disappeared. The presence
of profane elements in
a sacred painting, including
references to astrology,
reflects an intellectual
custom of the time and
is recurrent in Ferrarese
painting.

5

Giovanni Bellini
(Venice 1434/39–1516)
*5. Madonna Enthroned
Adoring the Sleeping Child*
Panel, 120 × 63 cm
Cat. 591
Acquisition: 1812,
following the suppressions
Latest restoration: 2000

Damaged at the top,
the painting is from the
Doge's Palace (Magistrate
of the Militia of the Sea),
and was perhaps the
central part of a larger group.
In this work of the 1470s,
Bellini again reveals
his attentive observation
of the contemporary
figurative culture: the pose
of the Madonna resembles
the one in the polyptych
by Bartolomeo Vivarini
(Room 23, cat. 615),
while the throne motif
is taken from the Mantegna
altarpiece of San Zeno
in Verona.

Giovanni Bellini
(Venice 1434/39–1516)
*6. Virgin and Child
with Saints Catherine
and Magdalene*
Panel, 58 × 107 cm
Cat. 613
Acquisition: 1850, from
the bequest of Felicita Renier
Latest restoration: 1997

Dated around 1500
(although some critics
place it at about ten years
earlier), this painting reflects
the influence of Leonardo
da Vinci in its treatment
of the relationship between
background and subject,
for example in how the side
lighting makes the figures
appear from the shadows.
Leonardo was in Venice
during the year 1500s,
sketching the portrait
of Isabella d'Este. An
interesting recent opinion
holds that the relationship
could be the reverse.
Adorned with jewels
and dressed with refined
elegance, the two saints
seem more like two young
Venetian patricians
than celestial creatures.
A workshop copy of
this piece is on display
in the Prado, Madrid.

6

7

Hans Memling
(Selingestadt am Main
ca. 1435/40–Bruges 1494)
7. *Portrait of a Young Man*
Panel, 26 × 20 cm
Cat. 586
Acquisition: 1856, by
purchase from the Manfrin
collection
Latest restoration: 1998

The portrait of the young
man with his hair arranged
in the "Italian" style is
exemplary of Memling's
portraiture. Viewed from
a three-quarters perspective
and cropped at the
shoulders, he is supported
to the right by an invisible
parapet in front of a
landscape with trees. His
pensive mien is revealed
by the frontal lighting, while
the sober clothing appears
black today, but was
originally a dark reddish
brown. Dates to around
1480 or shortly thereafter.

Giovanni Bellini
(Venice 1434/39–1516)
8. *Madonna and Child
with Saint John the Baptist
and Saint*
Panel, 55 × 77 cm
Cat. 881
Acquisition: 1926, from
the Giovanelli collection
by special agreement
with the State
Latest restoration: 1998

The work attests to the
artist's attempt at the
beginning of the 1500s
to insert figures taller than
the usual half-bust into a
more articulated space.
It also reveals numerous
corrections over the course
of the painting. The gestures,
the poses and the expressions
of the images in the
foreground prefigure the
Passion of the baby Jesus,
depicted with his feet already
crossed, just as they will be
on the cross. The landscape
in the background is full
of Marian symbols
such as the castle, the port,
the fortress and the
mountains, which—together
with the Christological
elements—were intended
to provoke the devout
oration of the faithful.

8

9

Giovanni Bellini
(Venice 1434/39–1516)
9. *Pietà*
Panel, 65 × 87 cm
Cat. 883
Acquisition: 1934, from
the Donà delle Rose
collection, following
an agreement
Latest restoration: 1996

A work commissioned
for private use, Bellini's
Pietà dates to the beginning
of the sixteenth century
and is signed near the
bottom on the left side.
It originally belonged

to the Martinengo family
who had it restored in 1866.
The most recent restoration
revealed the well preserved
paint. Careful analysis
of the meadow and the
image of Mary holding
her dead Son suggest the
influence of Dürer, or in
any case of Flemish culture.
Rich with religious
symbolism (including the
dry tree covered in ivy
and the small shrub
to the left of Christ, symbols
of Judaism and Christianity),
the background landscape
brings together buildings

of various locations
in suggestive synthesis,
including the pre-Palladian
basilica, the duomo and
the tower of Vicenza,
a view of the Natisone at
Cividale and the campanile
of Sant'Appollinare Nuovo
in Ravenna.

10

11

Giovanni Bellini
(Venice 1434/39–1516)
10. *Madonna and Child*
(*Madonna of the Red
Cherubs*)
Panel, 77 × 60 cm
Cat. 612
Acquisition: 1812,
following the suppressions
Latest restoration: 1995

Painted in the late 1400s,
this work was originally in
the Scuola della Carità. The
motif of the red cherubs,
burning with love, is taken
from the Pesaro *Coronation*
of 1474. In the background—
a luminous landscape rich
with Marian symbols such
as the hills, the river and the
fortified city—Mary stares
at her Son, almost enclosed
in her hands, with tender
awareness of his destiny.

Giovanni Bellini
(Venice 1434/39–1516)
11. *Virgin with Standing
Blessing Child*
Panel, 78 × 60 cm
Cat. 594
Acquisition: 1838,
by donation from
Girolamo Contarini
Latest restoration: 2000

This may be the same
Madonna that Taddeo

Contarini left to his relative
Girolamo in his will of 1578.
Dating to 1480, the piece was
created for private devotion
and was copied in many
variations by the master's
collaborators; Giovanni
himself would refer back
to it some years later in his
Madonna degli Alberetti.
In the background can be
seen the Torre di Piazza
in Vicenza, as it appeared
to people arriving from
Venice and Padua.

Giovanni Bellini
(Venice 1434/39–1516)
12. *Madonna and Child*
(*Madonna degli Alberetti*;
Madonna of the Trees)
Panel, 71 × 58 cm
Cat. 596
Acquisition: 1838,
by donation from
Girolamo Contarini
Latest restoration: 1998

The first dated work by
Giovanni Bellini (the date
1487 and Bellini's signature
can be seen near the bottom
in the center, almost as if
the foot of the small Jesus
is pointing to them).
The two trees at the sides,
for which the piece is named,
may allude to the *Song of
Songs*, or rather, given the

dry shrubs at the sides
of the trees, to the Old
and New Testaments.
The luminosity of the thin
bands of landscape, the
play between shadows
and light, and the posture

of the Mother allowing
the devotee to observe her
Son—barely covered by
her delicate hands—make
this one of the most
moving works for private
devotion.

12

13

Giorgio or Zorzi da Castelfranco known as Giorgione
(Castelfranco 1476/77–
Venice 1510)
13. *The Tempest*
Canvas, 82 × 73 cm
Cat. 915
Acquisition: 1932,
purchased from
Prince Alberto Giovanelli
Latest restoration: 1984

This painting has always
been identified with
"el paeseto in tela con la
tempesta con la cingana et
soldato, fu de man de Zorzi

di Castelfranco" ("the
landscape on canvas with the
gypsy and soldier in a storm,
by the hand of Giorgione
of Castelfranco"), mentioned
in 1530 by the historian
Marcantonio Michiel in
Gabriele Vendramin's
"camerino delle anticaglie"
(cabinet of antiques).
It is also indicated in an
inventory for Vendramin's
heirs in 1567–69, and
in another in 1601.
It was subsequently
purchased by the wealthy
merchant Cristoforo Orsetti
(*Figure di collezionisti*

2002), who refers to it in his
will of 1664. Left to his son
Salvatore, it ended up in the
hands of Girolamo Manfrin
at the end of the eighteenth
century. Its presence in
his collection was recorded
by writers and travelers
from the beginning of the
nineteenth century onward.
In 1875 it was acquired
by Prince Giovanelli.
X-ray and IR analyses have
revealed a nude woman
seated below the young man,
washing herself in the pool
of water to the left, and
numerous other small

corrections, especially in the
landscape. A work for private
enjoyment, *The Tempest* has
been the source of countless
interpretations, from
mythological to allegorical and
even political. It has also been
seen as the melding of many
literary and figurative sources,
or even as a work which would
not require any decoding
whatsoever, representing
simply what Michiel has
suggested: a "tempest"
with a gypsy. The dating
of the piece is also difficult,
although critics generally
place it around 1505/06.

14

**Giorgio or Zorzi
da Castelfranco known as
Giorgione**
(Castelfranco 1476/77–
Venice 1510)
14. *The Old Woman*
Canvas, transferred from
previous canvas, 68 × 59 cm
Cat. 272
Acquisition: 1856,
by acquisition from the
Manfrin collection
Latest restoration: 1984

Like *The Tempest*, *The Old
Woman* was also part of the
Vendramin collection, and
is quoted in its inventory

of 1567–69 and 1601. The
entry for 1601 also provides
a measurement of the frame,
which is still the original one.
It was later acquired by the
merchant Cristoforo Orsetti,
who mentions it in his last
will and testament of 1664
(*Figure di collezionisti*
2002), and was inherited
by his son Giovan Battista.
At an unknown date it
entered the Manfrin
collection. The interpretation
of this work is extremely
controversial: clearly an
allegory, judging by the
inscription "col tempo"

("with time") on the scroll,
it is an extraordinary
portrait. Dating to after
1505 and before 1508,
it seems to reflect certain
ideas of Leonardo da Vinci,
evident in the dark
background, the impious
analysis, but without turning
into caricature, the gesture
of the hand pointed towards
the chest, similar to that
of the apostle Philip
in Leonardo da Vinci's
Last Supper in Milan.

Room 13

Giovanni Bellini
(Venice 1434/39–1516)
15. *Scroll and Head of Christ*
Panels, 33 × 22 cm each
Cat. 87
Acquisition: 1838,
by donation from
Girolamo Contarini
Latest restoration: 1994

The two fragments
(the signature appears on
one) were probably part
of a *Transfiguration* or
Ascension. There used
to be a painting of the same
subject by the artist
in the chapel in Vicenza
Cathedral once dedicated
to the Transfiguration,
but it has now been lost.
A new kind of humanity can
be seen in the face of Christ,
bringing it closer to the
Baptism in Santa Corona,
Vicenza, created in the early
1500s.

Giovanni Bellini
(Venice 1434/39–1516)
16. *Allegorical Scenes*
Panels, 34 × 22 cm,
34 × 22 cm, 34 × 22 cm,
32 × 22 cm, 27 × 19 cm
Cat. 595
Acquisition: 1838,
by donation from
Girolamo Contarini
Latest restoration: 2000

The panels were probably
part of a piece of furniture
with a mirror, used for
holding toiletries. These
were so popular as to attract
the attention of the Senate,
which prohibited their
production with a decree
in 1489. The images that
decorated the pieces were
moral allegories. The woman
with the sphere is perhaps a
depiction of Melancholy or
fickle Fortune; the nude with
the mirror represents Vanity;
and the reflection may be of

the commissioner; the image
of Bacchus on a chariot
offering a plate of fruit to a
warrior is a reference to Lust,
tempting the virtuous man;
the allegory of Slander
or Envy is represented by
the panel with a seashell and
a man with a twisted snake.
The fifth panel—which was
probably part of a different
piece, or a replacement
of a lost part—has been
attributed to Andrea Previtali
(Bergamo 1470/80–1528).
It depicts blindfolded
Fortune, set between two
spheres, with two amphoras
containing pleasure
and anguish.
This iconography was
common in the Germanic
tradition. The critics do not
agree on the dates which
fluctuate between the late
1480s to the early 1500s,
the latter perhaps the
most probable.

15

16

16

16

16

16

129   **Room 13**

17

Jacopo da Ponte known as Jacopo Bassano
(Bassano ca. 1515–1592)
17. *Adoration of the Shepherds*
Canvas, 95 × 140 cm
Cat. 1360
Acquisition: 1983, by purchase

This may be the painting identified in 1620 in the Giusti del Giardino collection, indeed, the piece was purchased from Count Justo Giusti del Giardino himself. Nonetheless, Ridolfi also makes mention in 1648 of the existence of a very similar work in the house of Cristoforo Orsetti, in which Bassano was believed to imitate "the elegance of Padovanino." In this composition, which evokes Titian-like themes, there is a unique blend of Parmigianino influences (most evident in the image of the Virgin), mannerist refinement and naturalistic observations in the depiction of the animals and the faces of the shepherds. It dates to 1545 or shortly after.

18

19

Jacopo Robusti known as Jacopo Tintoretto
(Venice 1519–1594)
18. *Portrait of Procurator Jacopo Soranzo*
Canvas, 106 × 90 cm
Cat. 245
Acquisition: 1812, following the suppressions
Latest restoration: 1957

Painted for the Procuratoria de Supra, this work was originally in the form of a lunette, and to make it rectangular it was joined at the top—on the left with a triangular piece of canvas and on the right with a short strip to frame Soranzo. The alteration probably took place at the end of the 1500s, when many paintings were adapted by Tintoretto and his son Domenico for the new rooms of the rebuilt Procurators's Offices. The fragmentary writing carries the name of the subject and the date of 1522, which indicates when Soranzo took office and not when the painting was completed. The portrait is dated to around 1550, just after the portrait of Soranzo with a group of relatives, today at the Castello Sforzesco in Milan. Both paintings are from before 1551, however, the year the Procurator died. Despite its official "formal" use, the picture reveals a surprising expressive power.

Jacopo Robusti known as Jacopo Tintoretto)
(Venice 1519–1594)
19. *Portrait of Doge Alvise Mocenigo*
Canvas, 116 × 97 cm
Cat. 233
Acquisition: 1817, following the suppressions
Latest restoration: 1993

From the Procuratoria de Ultra, the office in Saint Mark's Square of the Procurators who dealt with the Basilica's holdings on the other side—"ultra"—of the Grand Canal. As with the preceding portrait, this one was originally in the form of a lunette, and depicts Alvise Mocenigo, who was born in 1507 and served as Doge from 1570 until 1577, the year the portrait was made, probably just after the election. In the noble pose and sober tonality can be seen the influence of the style of portraiture practiced by Titian, whom Tintoretto had succeeded as the official portrait artist of the Venetian Republic.

14 Seventeenth-Century Paintings

This room has undergone the same renovations as Room 13.

Annibale Carracci
Saint Francis, detail.

Annibale Carracci
(Bologna 1560–1609)
1. *Saint Francis*
Canvas, 91 × 73 cm
Cat. 1189
Acquisition: 1901,
by purchase
Latest restoration: 1955

An early work from around
1585–86—of which there
are copies in the Galleria
Nazionale in Rome and in
the Liechtenstein collection
in Vaduz—the painting
reflects in its great elegance
the influence of the major
Veneto painters of the 1500s.
The landscape is marvelous,
with its symbolic elements
which are equally valid as
still lifes in their own right.

1

Bernardo Strozzi
(Genoa 1581–Venice 1644)
2. *Saint Jerome*
Canvas, 56 × 47 cm
Cat. 424
Acquisition: 1838, by
donation from Girolamo
Contarini
Latest restoration: 1962

This devotional painting
of a theme repeated
many times by the artist
is generally attributed
to the early period
of Strozzi's stay in Venice,
around the 1640s.

2

Domenico Fetti
(Rome? 1588/89–
Venice 1623)
3. *Parable of the Good
Samaritan*
Canvas, 61 × 45 cm
Cat. 503
Acquisition: 1838,
by donation from
Girolamo Contarini
Latest restoration: 1948

"Parables" are among the
most common subjects
treated by Fetti, such as this
one of the good Samaritan,
like its preparatory drawing
at the Louvre (inv. 3069)
ca. 1617. There are various
replicas of the subject,
including the Gemäldegalerie
one in Dresden, in a
horizontal format.

3

Johann Liss
(Holstein ca. 1597–
Verona 1631)
4. *Apollo and Marsyas*
Canvas, 58 × 48 cm
Cat. 674
Acquisition: 1838,
by donation from
Girolamo Contarini

Among the last works
of the painter, who enriched
his early training in Rome
among the Dutch admirers
of Caravaggio with a
knowledge of Venetian
art gained during a stay
in Venice.

4

5

Domenico Fetti, copy from
(Rome? 1588/89–
Venice 1623)
5. *Portrait
of Francesco Andreini*
Canvas, 102 × 79 cm
Cat. 678
Acquisition: 1838,
by donation from
Girolamo Contarini
Latest restoration: 1956

A copy of the portrait of the
actor Francesco Andreini
(Pistoia ca. 1548–Mantua
1624) kept at the Hermitage
in Saint Petersburg.
This painting mimics
sixteenth-century Venetian
or Carracci-inspired models,
and dates to before 1620,
when Andreini left Mantua.
It depicts the subject with a
mask
in his hand, symbol of his
profession, and uniquely
recalls Eduardo De Filippo,
thereby obtaining further
depth, depicting not only
Francesco Andreini but
every actor, beyond every
limit of time.

Johann Liss
(Holstein ca. 1597–
Verona 1631)
6. *The Sacrifice of Isaac*
7. *Abel Mourned by His
Parents*
Canvases, 66 × 85 cm,
66 × 89 cm
Cats. 914, 913
Acquisition: 1932,
by purchase
Latest restoration: 1959

These paintings, purchased
from the Giovanelli
collection, date to the years
when the artist sojourned
in Venice (1624–29).
The dramatic effect
of the subject is diluted
in a powerful melancholy,
a result of the emphasis
given to the landscape
where the event is taking
place. *The Sacrifice* is one
of Liss' masterpieces;
there are other versions
of the second painting,
with variations.

6

7

Room 14

8

Domenico Fetti
(Rome? 1588/89–
Venice 1623)
8. *David with the Head
of Goliath*
Canvas, 175 × 128 cm
Cat. 669
Acquisition: 1838,
by donation from
Girolamo Contarini
Latest restoration: 1996

The painting came to the
Galleries from a descendent
of Giorgio Contarini dagli
Scrigni, a patron of Fetti
in Venice. It dates from
between 1617 and 1619, prior
to when the artist resided
in Venice. The young man,
with his indolent beauty
and contemporary dress,
harks to Caravaggio's elegant
knights in *Buona Ventura*

or the *Martyrdom of Saint
Matthew*. The face bears
some similarity to the
one used for the *David*
in Dresden (Gemäldegalerie)
and in Moscow (Pushkin
Museum).

9

Domenico Fetti
(Rome? 1588/89–
Venice 1623)
9. *Meditation*
Canvas, 179 × 140 cm
Cat. 671
Acquisition: 1838,
by donation from
Girolamo Contarini
Latest restoration: 1961

Although the donor
was a descendent of Giorgio
Contarini dagli Scrigni,
a patron of Fetti in Venice,
this famous painting
is believed to have been
completed around 1618,
before the artist actually
resided in Venice. The good
fortune of the piece is
evidenced by the numerous
copies and replicas. There

were also some illustrious
antecedents such as
Dürer's famous engraving,
Melancholy (1514), or
the *Vision of Saint Helena*
by Paolo Veronese, or the
Magdalene by Correggio.
In spite of the traditional
title, it is likely that
the artist kept in mind a part
of the second Letter of Paul
to the Corinthians 2 (7, 10),

which holds that Christian
"sadness" that produces
repentance leads to salvation,
while worldly "sadness"
brings on death. The female
figure is situated between
the still life of the lower part
of the painting alluding
to death and the "sadness
of the world." The grapevine
above symbolizes life and
salvation.

15 Giambattista Tiepolo, Pietro Longhi, Giannantonio Guardi and Giovanni Antonio Pellegrini

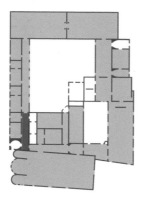

This is the final part of the long Palladio corridor. The "cell" structure (Rooms 16 and 16a) is to the left, while towards the interior of the building is a large exhibition space that was created from joining three rooms (into Room 17, currently closed for restoration); a door remains into one of these rooms. Towards the rear, through the large doorway, is found the famous oval stairway designed by Palladio in 1561. Here the works of Pietro Longhi, previously kept in Room 17, are exhibited.

Giannantonio Guardi
Herminia and Vaprinus Happen Upon the Wounded Tancredi after His Duel with Argante, detail.

1

4

2

3

Giambattista Tiepolo
(Venice 1696–Madrid 1770)
1. *Apparition of the Sacred
Family to Saint Gaetanus*
Canvas, 128 × 73 cm
Cat. 481
Acquisition: 1887,
by purchase
Latest restoration: 1970

Originally painted for the
altar of the small chapel
of Palazzo Labia in Venice.
The sacred image here
is conceived in a new way,
outside a classical building.
Dates to 1735–36.

Francesco Solimena
(Nocera dei Pagani 1657–
Barra 1747)
2. *Jacob and Rachel*
3. *Rebecca and the Servant
of Abraham*
Canvases, 198 × 150 cm,
202 × 150 cm
Cats. 871, 870
Acquisition: 1920,
by purchase
Latest restoration: 2008

These two paintings were
completed around 1710
for the Venetian home
of the Baglioni family
on Rio Marin, and were
then transferred, towards
middle of that century,
to the Palazzo Muti
in San Cassiano, where
they remained until their
purchase. The modeling
of the forms and vigorous
chiaroscuro contrasts were
surely noted by artists such
as Giambattista Piazzetta
and Giambattista Tiepolo
during their early activity.

Giambattista Tiepolo
(Venice 1696–Madrid 1770)
4. *Saint Joseph with the Baby
Jesus and Saints Francis
of Paola, Anne, Peter
of Alcantara and Anthony*
Canvas, 210 × 114 cm
Cat. 484
Acquisition: 1838,
following the suppressions
Latest restoration: 1960–61

This work was completed
in the early 1740s for the
church of the Benedictine
monks of San Prosdocimo
in Padua. It reveals the
continuing influence
of Piazzetta in the brownish
intonation of the color,
and in the compositional
structure.

Giambattista Pittoni
(Venice 1687–1767)
5. *Annunciation*
Canvas, 153 × 205 cm
Cat. 438
Acquisition: 1807,
from the old Accademia
Latest restoration: 1961

Painted in 1757 and
displayed in 1777 at
the Fiera della Sensa
(Feast of the Ascension),
after the death of the artist.
The work was painted
for the Assembly Hall
of the Accademia,
in its old location at the
Fonteghetto della Farina,
where Angeli and Marinetti
also assisted with the
decoration. Pittoni's
emphasis seems to have been
concentrated on the forms
in the composition, which
reveal notable stylistic
virtuosity.

5

Room 15

6

7

8

Giannantonio Guardi
(Vienna 1699–Venice 1760)
6. *Herminia and Vaprinus Happen Upon the Wounded Tancredi after His Duel with Argante*
Canvas, 250 × 261 cm
Cat. 1387
Acquisition: 1988, with the recoveries by Rodolfo Siviero

This canvas, recovered by Rodolfo Siviero in an English collection, is the only work by Guardi at the Accademia, and was probably part of a cycle of thirteen paintings originally in a villa in Este. The painting was inspired by an edition of Tasso's *Jerusalem Delivered* with engravings by Piazzetta at the height of his maturity, from around 1750–55. The engravings are now dispersed among various museums and collections abroad. The painting depicts a scene from the 19th canto of the epic poem, in close relation to the Piazzetta drawing at the Biblioteca Reale in Turin and its related engraving. Giannantonio's interpretation confers a fresh chromatic scheme, with light brush strokes, while a theatrical flair accentuates the typically Rococo musicality and easy grace of the composition.

Giovan Antonio Pellegrini
(Venice 1675–1741)
7. *Sculpture*
8. *Painting*
Canvases, 142 × 132 cm each
Cats. 1320, 1319
Acquisition: 1959, by purchase
Latest restoration: 1993

These two pendants depict the allegory of Painting and Sculpture. They are representative of Pellegrini's subtle elegance and refined use of color, the artist being one of the protagonists of the international Rococo, the brother-in-law of Rosalba Carriera. Close in style to the altarpiece with the *Healing of the Cripple* at the Karlskirche in Vienna, they can be dated to 1728.

9

Angelo Trevisani
(Treviso? 1669–1753/55)
9. *Expulsion of the Merchants from the Temple*
Canvas, 121 × 201 cm
Cat. 790
Acquisition: 1912, by purchase
Latest restoration: 1960

This is the draft, with notable variations, of the large painting made by the artist in 1732 for the Venetian church of Santi Cosma e Damiano on Giudecca island. After the suppressions it was transferred to Milan, and from 1818 it was kept in the parish church of Somaglia (Lodi).

Giandomenico Tiepolo
(Venice 1727–1804)
10. *Abraham and the Angels*
Canvas, 200 × 281 cm
Cat. 834
Acquisition: 1807, following the suppressions
Latest restoration: 2007

This is the last painting commissioned by the Scuola della Carità to complete the decoration of the hall of the new Chancellery, erected in 1764. A contest was held for this purpose, whose theme turned on the "Return of the Prodigal Son" with entrants sending drafts to a Roman academy commission which included Anton Raffaele Mengs. Giandomenico

won the competition, and on March 8, 1773, he began the work for a total of 116 *zecchini* (sequins). A drawing by Giambattista at the State Museum of Berlin appears to have been a counterpart of this piece; the group of angels recalls one painted by his father of the same subject in the Prado, while the figure of Abraham is inspired by the painting in the Luna-Villahermosa collection in Madrid. There are three preparatory studies for Abraham by Giandomenico at the Museo Correr. The smoothness of the color and the cold purity of the drawing are early reflections of neoclassical thought.

10

Room 15

11

Pietro Longhi
(Venice 1701–1785)
11. *The Tailor*
Canvas, 60 × 49 cm
Cat. 469
Acquisition: 1838,
by donation from Girolamo
Contarini
Latest restoration: 1995

In spite of the traditional
title, this is actually a group
portrait, as is shown by
the image of the Procurator
Nicolò Renier, elected in
1740, hanging on the wall.
Samaritana Dolfin, the wife
of Girolamo, Nicolò Renier's
brother, has just received
the tailor, with a magnificent
new dress; next to her
the daughter Maria plays
with the dog.
Dating to after *The Concert*,
between 1742–43, this piece
came to the Galleries from
the Contarini collection.

Pietro Longhi
(Venice 1701–1785)
12. *The Concert*
Canvas, 60 × 49 cm
Cat. 466
Acquisition: 1838,
by donation from
Girolamo Contarini
Latest restoration: 1995

Signed and dated "Pietro
Longhi, 1741," this painting
is a masterpiece revealing the
transition from the popular
form derived from Giuseppe
Maria Crespi to the more
refined "conversation piece"
taken from the French
tradition. The work confirms
Longhi's place as a "painter
of the Veneto nobility."
Some clergymen play cards
in a suggestive patrician
room, while the owners
of the house are arranged
in an unusual trio of only
violinists.

12

13

Pietro Longhi
(Venice 1701–1785)
13. *The Apothecary*
Canvas, 59 × 48 cm
Cat. 467
Acquisition: 1838, by donation
from Girolamo Contarini
Latest restoration: 1995

With the artist's signature
on the back, this is probably
his most famous painting.

The interior is described in
such intricate detail that the
Nativity painting by Antonio
Balestra can be recognized,
a work now in a private
collection in Venice. Longhi
evokes an eighteenth-century
chemist's shop with
remarkable success.
The piece dates to around the
same time as *The Rhinoceros*
in Ca' Rezzonico, from 1751.

14

Pietro Longhi
(Venice 1701–1785)
14. *Lady at Her Toilette*
Canvas, 60 × 48 cm
Cat. 464
Acquisition: 1838,
by donation from
Girolamo Contarini
Latest restoration: 1995

The focus of the composition
is the splendid dress worn
by the lady, which shows
that the dressing ritual
was an important moment in
the day of eighteenth-century
Venetian patrician women.
From around the same time
as *The Concert*.

Pietro Longhi
(Venice 1701–1785)
15. *The Dancing Lesson*
Canvas, 60 × 48 cm
Cat. 465
Acquisition: 1838,
by donation from
Girolamo Contarini
Latest restoration: 1995

A famous painting which
was made diffuse through
a counterpart engraving
by Flipart. The work depicts
one of the fundamental
aspects of the education
of young Venetian patrician
girls, and dates to around
the 1740s or 50s.

Pietro Longhi
(Venice 1701–1785)
16. *The Fortune Teller*
Canvas, 60 × 48 cm
Cat. 468
Acquisition: 1838,
by donation from
Girolamo Contarini
Latest restoration: 1995

The inscription, top right
"Per Piovan / in San Fantin /
pre' Zuanne," probably refers
to the parochial election in
San Fantin of don Giovanni
(Zuanne) Pecchion, which
occurred on August 6, 1759,
the *post quem* date for the
completion of this piece.

16

15

16 Early Works by Giambattista Tiepolo, Sebastiano Ricci, Bernardo Bellotto, Marco Ricci, Michele Marieschi, Francesco Guardi and Canaletto

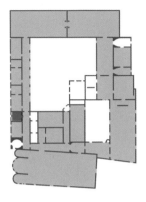

This room has the same original dimensions
of the convent cell. It was remodeled
by Carlo Scarpa in 1947; later, in 1959,
he also designed the support for Piazzetta's
Fortune Teller.
Some of the works from Room 17, currently
closed for restoration, are temporarily
exhibited in this room.

Giambattista Tiepolo
Rape of Europa, detail.

Sebastiano Ricci
(Belluno 1659–Venice 1734)
1. *Diana and Callisto*
Canvas, 64 × 76 cm
Cat. 1383
Acquisition: 1988, with the
recoveries by Rodolfo Siviero

This work was originally
in a private British collection,
then in the Contini
Bonacossi collection in
Florence. It was purchased
in 1941 by Göring, who took
it to Germany from where
it was recovered by Rodolfo
Siviero in 1948. Inspired
by Ovid's *Metamorphoses*;
this painting depicts the
moment when Diana points
at Callisto, who was guilty of
having been seduced by Jove.
This composition, appearing
almost neoclassical, was
also sketched on a sheet
in the Galleries. With its
elegant use of color, the work
is attributed to the English
period of the artist's career,
from 1712–16.

1

Sebastiano Ricci
(Belluno 1659–Venice 1734)
2. *Bacchanal in Honor of Pan*
Canvas, 84 × 100 cm
Cat. 1384
Acquisition: 1988, with the
recoveries by Rodolfo Siviero

This painting, previously
in the Detsy collection, passed
over to the Voss collection
of Wiesbaden and then
to the Barsanti's in Rome.
It was later exported to
Germany, where it was
recovered by Rodolfo Siviero
in 1956. Studied in numerous
drawings kept in the royal
collections of Windsor
and the Accademia Galleries,
the piece dates to 1716, after
Ricci's brief stay in Paris
while returning from London.
The circular movement visible
in this painting conveys the
drunkenness of the bacchanal
in honor of Pan, the deity
with the horns and the goat's
hooves, lover of dance,
music and wine.

2

3

5

4

6

Giambattista Tiepolo
(Venice 1696–Madrid 1770)
3. *Rape of Europa*
4. *Diana and Acteon*
5. *Apollo and Marsyas*
6. *Diana and Callisto*
Canvases, 100 × 135 cm each
Cats. 435, 440, 711, 712
Acquisition: 1898, by
purchase *Rape of Europa* and
Diana and Acteon; 1907,
by purchase for the other two
paintings
Latest restoration: 1993

On the first canvas is
depicted Europa, the
daughter of the Phoenician
king Agenor, who was taken
to Crete by Jove disguised
as a bull, where she gave
birth to Minos. On the
second canvas is Acteon,
who is changed to a stag
after seeing Diana bathing
nude; he is then torn
to pieces by his own
hunting dogs. In the third
is represented the musical
contest between Apollo
and Pan; Midas is already
depicted with ass's ears,

the punishment he received
for not picking Apollo as
the winner. On the last
painting Diana discovers
that the huntress Callisto
has been seduced by Zeus.
Chased away by Diana,
she then gives birth to Arcas
and is changed by Hera
into a bear. Later her son will
find her and almost kill her,
but Zeus intervenes, changing
both into constellations. The
four paintings—identical in
format and style—are inspired
by Ovid's *Metamorphoses*.
Acquired a few years apart
in Belluno, the pieces were
part of a decorative series,
probably in a Belluno
palazzo. They are early works
by the artist, from around
1720–21, when Tiepolo
was about to abandon
the dark and dramatic
tones and lighten his palette,
demonstrating a new
ability to articulate figures
within space.

Room 16

8

Bernardo Bellotto
(Venice 1721–Warsaw 1780)
7. *Rio dei Mendicanti
and the Scuola Grande
di San Marco*
Canvas, 41 × 59 cm
Cat. 494
Acquisition: 1856, from
the Manfrin collection
Latest restoration: 1990

This is probably the painting
alluded to by Ruskin when
he described himself painting
the scene from the same
viewpoint, but in opposition
to Canaletto. Nonetheless,
by now the work is largely
attributed to Bellotto
while in his apprenticeship
in the studio of his uncle,
Canaletto; the work dates
to around 1740 and its
success is confirmed
by the numerous copies
that were made of it.

**Antonio Canal known as
Canaletto and Workshop**
(Venice 1697–1768)
8. *Capriccio with Ruins
and Porta Portello in Padua*
9. *Capriccio with Ruins
and Classical Buildings*
Canvases, 61 × 76 cm,
62 × 74 cm
Cats. 1385, 1386
Acquisition: 1988
Latest restoration: 1993

The first canvas comes
from the Contini-Bonacossi
collection in Florence.
The work was removed
in a clandestine operation
and then recovered
by Rodolfo Siviero.
There are twenty-two copies
of this *Capriccio*, which
received enormous praise.
The copies are attributed
to Canaletto and Bellotto's
circle. The version in the
Kunsthalle in Hamburg
is probably the model
upon which they were based.
The excellent version in
Venice is from Canaletto's
work around the 1760s.

A pendant of the first
painting, *Capriccio
with Ruins and Classical
Buildings* underwent
a similar situation.
The constructions depicted
in the work seem to all be
of the artist's imagination,
although they may bring
known buildings to mind.
There are sixteen replicas
of this subject; the model
on which these were based
has been recognized as the
version in the Poldi-Pezzoli
museum in Milan.
Comparison between
the one here in Venice and
the one in Milan reveals
that the Venetian version
is actually better, with
more luminous colors and
a clear descriptive analysis.

9

10

10

Antonio Canal known as Canaletto
(Venice 1697–1768)
10. *Capriccio of a Colonnade*
Canvas, 130 × 92 cm
Cat. 463
Acquisition: 1807, from
the old Accademia
Latest restoration: 1985

Trial work of acceptance
after the artist was made
professor of perspective
architecture, signed and
dated 1765. The painting,
now famous and copied
many times by Canaletto
himself, was exhibited in
1777 in Saint Mark's Square
for the Fiera della Sensa
(Feast of the Ascension).
A drawing in the Albertini
collection in Rome is
related to the painting,
and a quick sketch in
Museo Correr could be
an early idea for the piece.

Francesco Guardi
(Venice 1712–1793)
11. *Saint Mark's Basin
with the Island of San
Giorgio and the Giudecca*
Canvas, 69 × 94 cm
Cat. 709
Acquisition: 1903, by
donation from Prince John
of Liechtenstein
Latest restoration: 1993

On the crate of the boat
at the bottom right is
the signature: "F.G." This
is one of a many versions
of a theme treated numerous
times by the artist. To the
left the island of San Giorgio
Maggiore, and to the right
the Giudecca island with
the demolished church
of San Giovanni Battista
of the Camaldolesi monks,
and the church of the Zitelle.
The painting maintains
its expressive potential
in spite of a certain
graininess in the color.
It is from no later than 1774,
when the old onion-domed
bell tower on the island
of San Giorgio, still present
in this painting, collapsed.

11

12

Francesco Guardi
(Venice 1712–1793)
12. *Fire at San Marcuola*
Canvas, 32 × 51 cm
Cat. 1344
Acquisition: 1972,
by exercise of purchase right
Latest restoration: 1993

This is Guardi's rendering
of a real event: the dramatic
fire at the oil storehouse
in the Ghetto, which
occurred on November 28,
1789. It is among the
artist's masterpieces within
the documentary style,
composed towards his late
maturity.

13

14

Marco Ricci
(Belluno 1676–Venice 1730)
13. *Landscape with
Woodsmen and Knights*
14. *The Park of a Villa*
Goat skins,
29 × 45 cm, 30 × 44 cm

Cats. 1308, 1307
Acquisition: 1956,
from Palazzo Reale

Painted in tempera
on goat skin—a technique
that creates an effect

of extraordinary luminosity—
these two pendants date
to just before 1724. They
were were probably
originally located in the
monastery of San Giorgio.
The second painting,

with its evocation
of aspects of the daily
work of a patrician villa,
is a forerunner of the great
Vedutisti (view painters).

15

16

Michele Marieschi
(Venice 1710–1743)
15. *Capriccio with a Classical Arch and Goats*
16. *Capriccio with a Gothic Building and an Obelisk*

Canvases, 55 × 83 cm each
Cats. 727, 728
Acquisition: 1903,
by purchase
Latest restoration: 1962 for cat. 728; 1997 for cat. 727

These two pendants are highly original and refined works. The small speckles remind the viewer of the work of Giannantonio Guardi. Other versions

by the artist and his workshop exist of these paintings, and especially of the second one.

17

Giambattista Tiepolo
(Venice 1696–Madrid 1770)
17. *The Discovery of the True Cross and Saint Helena*
Canvas, 51 × 49 cm
Cat. 789
Acquisition: 1913,
by purchase from
Generoso Añes of Toledo
Latest restoration: 1985

This is the preparatory draft—or rather an early idea—for the large canvas by Tiepolo originally on the ceiling of the church of the Cappuccine in Castello (now in Room 11, cat. 462). The piece is characterized by a rapid, rotating movement that is somewhat more tranquil in the final version. Dates to around 1740.

Giambattista Tiepolo
(Venice 1696–Madrid 1770)
18. *Institution of the Rosary*
Canvas, 108 × 51.5 cm
Cat. 2020
Acquisition: 2006,
from the bequest
of Bianca De Feo Leonardi

The work, which formerly belonged to the Crespi collection in Milan, is one of three preparatory sketches for the central fresco in the vault of the church of Santa Maria del Rosario (Gesuati) in Venice, on which Tiepolo worked between 1737 and 1739. The theme celebrates two moments in the life of Saint Dominic: the institution of the Rosary, received from the Virgin, and the start of his Marian preaching.

18

Giambattista Tiepolo
(Venice 1696–Madrid 1770)
19. *The Glory of Saint Dominic*
Canvas, 78 × 72 cm
Cat. 810
Acquisition: 1922,
by purchase
Latest restoration: 1992–93

A draft painted for the competition for the ceiling of the chapel of San Domenico in the Basilica of Santi Giovanni e Paolo in March of 1723. This contest was won by Giambattista Piazzetta.

20. **Giambattista Tiepolo**
(Venice 1696–Madrid 1770)
Transfer of the Holy House of Nazareth
Canvas, 126 × 86 cm
Cat. 911
Acquisition: 1930,
by purchase
Latest restoration: 1993–94

A preparatory sketch for the ceiling and fresco painted by Tiepolo and Girolamo Mengozzi, known as Colonna, in the church of Santa Maria di Nazareth at the Scalzi, which was destroyed in 1915 by an Austrian bomb (seven surviving fragments are on display in Room 11, cats. 1376, 1378, 1377 and 836, 1375, 837, 1374). This is probably the first model for the composition, for which the artist was paid 100 *zecchini* on September 13, 1743. The second model, which is more similar to the final version, is at the Getty Museum in Malibu, California. The piece celebrates the miraculous conveyance of the house of Nazareth, where the Virgin encountered the angel Gabriel, to Loreto.

19

20

16a Alessandro Longhi, Giambattista Piazzetta, Fra' Galgario and Rosalba Carriera

This room, like the previous Room 16,
maintains the same original dimensions
of the convent cell. Both rooms were
remodeled by Carlo Scarpa in 1947.
In this room the pastels of Rosalba Carriera,
formerly in Room 17 which is closed
for restoration, are temporarily exhibited.

Giambattista Piazzetta
The Fortune Teller, detail

1

Giuseppe Angeli
(Venice 1712–1798)
1. *The Tickle*
Canvas, 198 × 144 cm
Cat. 1459
Acquisizione: 1995,
by purchase
Latest restoration: 1995–96

The work was acquired
on the Berlin antiquarian
market and then passed
into the Pospisil collection
in Venice. In 1990 it was
added to the collection
of Silvestro Gargantini
in Milan, from whom it
was purchased by the State
for the Venetian Gallery.
A student of Piazzetta, in this
work Angeli imitates similar
compositions by his master,
such as *The Fortune Teller*.
The Pastoral Scene by
Domenico Maggiotto
(Hamburg, Kunsthalle)
is another tickling scene,
confirming this subject
was common in Piazzetta's
milieu. There exists
a preparatory sketch,
bearing a dedication
with the date 1745, the year
to which our painting
can also be ascribed.

2

Giambattista Piazzetta
(Venice 1683–1754)
2. *The Fortune Teller*
Canvas, 154 × 115 cm
Cat. 483
Acquisition: 1887
Latest restoration: 1983

Acquired from the merchant
Ehrenfreund, on the back
of the original canvas there
was a leaf of paper with
the date of 1740, written
in eighteenth-century

handwriting, which was
widely accepted by critics.
This is one of the artist's
most famous works, and is
the culmination of his studies
on the "pastoral" theme
begun many years earlier,
first with the *Pastoral Scene*
(The Art Institute, Chicago),
and the *Idyll on the Beach*
(Wallraf-Richartz Museum,
Cologne). Both of these
paintings were commissioned
by Marshal Schulenburg,

who lived in Venice and was
a strong admirer of the artist.
The three works come from
that joyful period of clear
and bright colors that
contemporaries defined
as "lume solivo" (sunny light).
This painting is universally
called *The Fortune Teller*,
a title suggested by the pose
of the woman to the left
who seems to point to
the other woman's hand, but
its interpretations vary widely:

it can be seen politically,
symbolically or even as an
amorous initiation of the two
youths to the right, or of one
of them. The fascination
instilled by *The Fortune Teller*
consists in its subtle grace, the
sensual light that inundates
the piece, the extremely
refined chromatic harmony,
the serene wisdom of the
woman at the center, who, in
spite of her rustic garments is
a "sister" of Tiepolo's heroines.

Room 16a

**Vittore Ghislandi
(Fra' Galgario)**
(Bergamo 1655–1743)
3. *Portrait of Count
Giovanni Battista Vailetti*
Canvas, 230 × 137 cm
Cat. 778
Acquisition: 1912,
by purchase
Latest restoration: 1995

Purchased from A. Olivotti
through the Export Office
of Florence. This piece from
1710 was previously in the
collection of the Countess
Rosa Piatti Lochis, and
belonged to her family
for at least the latter half
of the nineteenth century
and bequeathed by the
family of Luigi Vailetti.
One of the most famous
portraits by the artist,
datable to the second decade
of the eighteenth century,
it constitutes a true
"still life with precious fabrics."
Perhaps because of his
Lombard origin, Ghislandi
moved away from the
frivolous and formal style
of international portraiture,
and instead gave Count
Vailetti—portrayed
in the refined intimacy of
his study—an interpretation
which was both idealized
and realistic at the same
time, with the proper rigor
of an illuminist.

Giuseppe Nogari
(Venice 1699–1763)
4. *An Old Woman
with a Bowl*
Canvas, 52 × 41 cm
Cat. 1315
Acquisition: 1953,
by donation from
Francesco Pospisil
Latest restoration: 1998

Alessandro Longhi's master,
Nogari specialized in the
production of "character
heads" realized with
chiaroscuro contrasts
and counter-lighting effects,
inspired by the Nordic
tradition. *An Old Woman
with a Bowl* dates to the
beginning of the 1740s
and is a virtuoso variation
of two paintings of the
Old Woman with a Staff:
one at the Gemäldegalerie
in Dresden, and the other
at the Prado Museum.

Alessandro Longhi
(Venice 1733–1813)
5. *The Family of Procurator of St. Mark's Luigi Pisani*
Canvas, 255 × 340 cm
Cat. 1355
Acquisition: 1979,
by purchase
Latest restoration: 1996

On the globe is written "Longhj," and on the upper border of the pages of the book below to the right is the original though fragmented signature "Alessandro Abate." Again to the lower right, the inscription "opus pietro longi." The work—inherited by the Bentivoglio of Aragon family and later by the Nani Mocenigo family—was carried out in 1758 together with a pendant (of which a fragment remains at the City Museum of Belluno, and which depicted the family of Ermolao Alvise and Andrea Pisani).

This painting shows Doge Alvise Pisani (1664–1741) with his son Luigi the procurator, his wife Paolina Gambara and four children surrounded by allegorical figures symbolizing family virtues. The two personages in the back to the right are probably two other children of the Pisani family, while the old man dressed in black who holds a "bussolà" (a Venetian cookie) towards the boy is probably the Abbot Giovanni Gregoretti. The allegorical figures around them allude to various family virtues; to the upper right can be seen the villa of Stra. Longhi emphasizes the small slices of the father Paolo's life in Venice, adding a psychological investigation to make the work one of the most suggestive examples of European portraiture of the time.

4

5

6

Alessandro Longhi
(Venice 1733–1813)
6. *Portrait of Carlo Lodoli*
Canvas, 128 × 94 cm
Cat. 908
Acquisition: 1930,
by donation from
Count A. di Robilant
Latest restoration: 1994

The painting carries
the signature and name
of the subject at the upper
left: the Franciscan
monk Carlo Lodoli
(Venice 1690–1761),
the famous theoretician
of the new architectural
rationalism, opposed

to the Baroque excesses
and a vehement critic
of many of his contemporary
architects. His pitiless
approach must have
garnered him quite a few
enemies, and in fact the
inscription expresses an
ironic criticism of him.
Longhi made more than one
portrait of this controversial
figure. The chronology
of this particular work
is difficult, although
it was surely posthumous.
It should be from around
the end of the 1770s, given its
similarity with the portrait
of Bartolomeo Ferracina
in Ca' Rezzonico, which
is from about 1770.

Rosalba Carriera
(Venezia 1673–1758)
7. *Portrait of the Daughter
of the Consul Le Blond*
Paper, 34 × 27 cm
Cat. 444
Acquisition: 1888,
from the bequest
of Vincenzo Omoboni Astori

The beginning of work
on the portrait is annotated
by Rosalba in her diary
for May 13, 1725. On July 22
she added, "Received from
the ambassador of France
a snuffbox with ten sequins,"
probably payment for the
work. The pastel technique
is remarkably well suited

to evoke the girl's tender
charm, grasped with
a delicate analysis which
depicts her refined dress,
the pink bow in her hair,
the lace scarf knotted around
her neck and the "bussolà,"
a traditional Venetian
cookie, which she is
clutching in her hand.

Rosalba Carriera
(Venezia 1673–1758)
8. *Portrait of the Son
of the Consul Le Blond*
Paper, 34 × 27 cm
Cat. 445
Acquisition: 1888, from
the bequest of Vincenzo
Omoboni Astori
Latest restoration: 1990

This portrait, like its
pendant, *Portrait of the
Daughter of the Consul
Le Blond*, depicts a son
of the French consul.
Painted by 1726, immediately
after that of the sister,
it is an image of charm
and exquisite courtesy.

7

8

9

Rosalba Carriera
(Venice 1673–1758)
9. *Portrait of a Young Nobleman*
Paper, 58 × 47 cm
Cat. 491
Acquisition: 1816, by bequest from Girolamo Molin

With a masterful use of pastels—which were made for the artist in Rome by her friend Christian Cole—Carriera creates images almost without any preparatory drawing, giving the piece unusual luminosity thanks to her use of a dark blue paper. This portrait dates to 1727, and is perhaps the son of Girolamo Zuan Francesco, born in 1702.

Room 16a

10

Rosalba Carriera
(Venice 1673–1758)
10. *Portrait of the Abbot
Dionisio Le Blond*
Paper, 57 × 45 cm
Cat. 486
Acquisition: 1888,
from the bequest
of Vincenzo Omoboni Astori

On July 23, 1729, Dionisio
Le Blond, then in Rome with

the Cardinal of Polignac,
wrote to Rosalba to express
his pleasure at the arrival
of a "beau tableau" which
seemed to have awakened
in the cardinal the desire
to have one like it. Scholars
have seen this as a reference
to the portrait of the
abbé and that of Polignac,
which would therefore
date from about 1729–30.

But if that were the case,
it is not clear why the
portrait of the cardinal
should have flowed into
the Astori bequest. Instead
it is likely that the portrait
appears in Rosalba's diary
entry for September 23,
1727: "Received from
the Consul of France sixty
sequins for the Cardinal,"
and dates from the same

year, together with the
portrait of the consul's
secretary and brother.
The latter is a masterpiece
of exceptional optical
fineness which achieves
an unusual realism.

11

Rosalba Carriera
(Venice 1673–1758)
11. *Self-Portrait*
Canvas, 31 × 25 cm
Cat. 907
Acquisition: 1927, through
a purchase option from
the Naya Company
Latest restoration: 1998

This painting was made by
the artist a few years before
she fell victim to "a total loss
of reason"; she would call the
piece a "tragedy," meaning
"that Rosalba would end
tragically." Compared with
the similar subject in the
English collections, Carriera's
face appears pained and
tired, almost foreshadowing
the real blindness that would
afflict the painter in 1746.

17 Currently closed for restoration

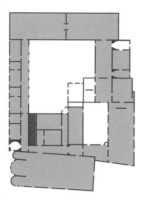

This room was fitted between 1921 and 1923
for the display of small eighteenth-century
paintings; in 1947 Carlo Scarpa added
small narrow gallery, with a typical Venetian
floor and a single velarium on the ceiling.
Currently closed for restoration,
the paintings are temporarily exhibited
in the adjoining rooms.

Pietro Longhi
Lady at Her Toilette, detail.

18 Trial Works by the Academicians and Models by Antonio Canova

This hallway was constructed in the early nineteenth century and redesigned by Carlo Scarpa in 1953. He closed off two windows and inserted a single door leading to a hanging terrace dating back to the 1940s and now removed to make way for the elevators and a new staircase. The wooden base was eliminated, the ceiling lowered and new skylights were opened.

The display cases with the Canova sketches were added in 1949. Originally the room was to be used for displaying a rotation of drawings, but later trial works from the old Accademia at the Fonteghetto della Farina were added.

Antonio Maria Visentini
Architectural Invention, detail.

1

Giuseppe Zais
(Canale d'Agordo 1709–
Treviso 1781)
1. *Landscape with
a Fountain*
Canvas, 132 × 80 cm
Cat. 447
Acquisition: 1807,
from the old Accademia
Latest restoration: 1962

On the bottom left are
the artist's initials.
With this painting
he applied, in 1765, to be
accepted into the Accademia,
but was not admitted until
September 11, 1774.

Francesco Battaglioli
(Modena 1714–recorded
until 1789)
2. *Architectural Perspective*
Canvas, 131 × 56 cm
Cat. 461
Acquisition: 1807,
from the old Accademia
Latest restoration: 1987

Chosen in 1777 with other
canvases from the old
Accademia to be exhibited
at the Fiera della Sensa
in Piazza San Marco.
The painting was completed
by Battaglioli to mark his
nomination to the Accademia
in 1776. The inventive work
reveals talents for perspective
and his familiarity with
Canaletto's work.

Giuseppe Moretti
(Val Camonica, active in
Venice during the second
half of the eighteenth
century)
3. *Perspective Study*
Canvas, 130 × 56 cm
Cat. 471
Acquisition: 1807,
from the old Accademia
Latest restoration: 1987

Displayed at the Fiera della
Sensa in 1777, this painting
was submitted by Moretti
for his entrance into
the Accademia in 1776.
Canaletto's influence is evident,
especially in the figures that
recall those in the *Campo
San Giacomo at Rialto* at the
Staatliche Museen of Berlin.

2

3

Pietro Gaspari
(Venice 1720–1785)
4. *Architectural Perspective*
Canvas, 131 × 79 cm
Cat. 470
Acquisition: 1807,
from the old Accademia
Latest restoration: 1987

To the lower left on the base
is the signature and the date
of 1775. This is the "pièce
de reception" for Gaspari's
acceptance into the
Accademia, and is a good
representation of virtuosity
of the "perspective" trend
in the 1700s.

Antonio Joli
(Modena ca. 1700–
Naples 1777)
5. *Perspective with Ancient
Baths*
Canvas, 130 × 93 cm
Cat. 450
Acquisition: 1807, from
the old Accademia
Latest restoration: 1987

"Pièce de reception"
for Joli's acceptance into the
Accademia, to which he was
elected on February 13, 1756,
this is a typical example of
the artist's painting. After
working as a scene painter
in Modena until about 1740,
he went to Venice to become
one of the major exponents
of "perspective" painting,
working also in Germany,
London and Madrid.

Antonio Maria Visentini
(Venice 1688–1782)
6. *Architectural Invention*
Canvas, 135 × 94 cm
Cat. 448
Acquisition: 1807,
from the old Accademia

The signature is written
at the left on the edge
of the balustrade. A group
of architects intent on
measuring the ruins of an
ancient building stand in a
portico that recalls Veronese
and Palladio. Their very
presence, along with the
drawing tools, the plumb
line, Palladio's *Trattato* at
easy reach, all allude to the
teaching of architectural
perspective as an essential
element of painting. The
work was connected with the
institution of the Perspective
Chair at the Accademia,
to which Visentini was
appointed in 1764, but which
was only confirmed in 1772.
The work was probably
completed after this date,
and is recorded in 1777,
when it was displayed
at the Fiera della Sensa.

4

5

6

Room 18

7

8

9

10

Domenico Fedeli known as Maggiotto
(Venice 1713–1794)
7. *Allegory of the Academy*
Canvas, 130 × 92 cm
Cat. 433
Acquisition: 1807,
from the old Accademia
Latest restoration: 1960

The signature is to the lower right. This painting was probably donated to the Accademia in 1763. The artist was admitted to the Accademia in 1756; this work is significant for its refined academic nature, in which Maggiotto effectively translates the teachings of Piazzetta.

Michelangelo Morlaiter
(Venice 1729–1806)
8. *Venice Awards the Fine Arts*
Canvas, 131 × 183 cm
Cat. 425
Acquisition: 1807,
from the old Accademia
Latest restoration: 1960

Displayed at the Fiera della Sensa in 1777, the work had most likely been donated to the Accademia in 1756 by Morlaiter when he was admitted. The figure of Venice is depicted awarding prize-medals to Painting, Sculpture and Architecture. The "academic" subject echoes a neoclassical aspect.

Francesco Maggiotto
(Venice 1750–1805)
9. *Allegory of Painting*
Canvas, 130 × 115 cm
Cat. 442
Acquisition: 1807,
from the old Accademia
Latet restoration: 1960

The signature is to the right on the sheet under the palette. The work was the obligatory donation made by the artist in 1769 for his election into the Accademia in 1768. While the seated woman symbolizes Painting, the standing woman is an allegory for Nature. The boy to the right represents Drawing. The influence of new neoclassical theories is evident in the work.

Pietro Longhi
(Venice 1701–1785)
10. *The Philosopher Pythagoras*
Canvas, 130 × 91 cm
Cat. 479
Acquisition: 1807, from the old Accademia

11

13

The signature is written at the lower left. The title is the one used by Pietro's son Alessandro for the engraving that reproduces his father's painting. The work was an entrance piece for the Accademia, which selected Longhi in its first group of students in February of 1756. Between the end of 1762 and the first months of 1763, it appears that—following their recall in May of 1761—on November 14, 1762, it was decided to send the canvases back to Longhi and to the other painters who had not yet completed the work required by the statute, with the injunction that the works were to be finished within six months. Longhi's position as an instructor on painting nudes evidently influenced his choice of subject.

Francesco Zuccarelli
(Pitigliano 1702–Florence ca. 1788)
11. *Landscape with the Young John the Baptist*
Canvas, 132 × 94 cm
Cat. 458
Acquisition: 1807, from the old Accademia
Latest restoration: 1960

Zuccarelli was elected into the Accademia on January 16, 1763, and at the same time was also chosen to be an instructor.

12

The painting was originally in the old Accademia, and must have been completed immediately after his appointment. Although the figure of John the Baptist appears conventional, the landscape reveals intense pictorial accents.

Pierantonio Novelli
(Venice 1729–1804)
12. *Drawing, Color and Invention*
Canvas, 130 × 132 cm
Cat. 762

Acquisition: 1807, from the old Accademia
Latest restoration: 1993

At the bottom-right is the inscription with the signature and date of 1776. Admitted into the Accademia in 1768, Novelli submitted this neoclassical-inspired work in 1771 and revised it again in 1776.

Alessandro Longhi
(Venice 1733–1813)
13. *Painting and Merit*
Canvas, 128 × 93 cm

Cat. 493
Acquisition: 1807, from the old Accademia
Latest restoration: 1958

The signature is painted on the spine of the book. This allegorical painting refers to the artist's acceptance into the Accademia in 1759 but dates to the end of the 1770s. The artist made an engraving of the painting and dedicated it to John Udny, the English Consul in Venice in 1761 and from 1773 to 1775.

14

Antonio Canova
(Possagno 1757–Venice 1822)
14. *Fighters*
Terracotta, 30 × 31 cm
Cat. 549
Acquisition: 1807,
from the old Accademia
Latest restoration: 1979

The signature is painted
on the base. With this group
from 1775, Canova won
second prize at the first
sculpture competition held
by the Accademia. The
subject is taken from the old
plaster copy in the Filippo
Farsetti collection (which
was, at the time, generously
made available to the
students); the original
is in the Uffizi in Florence.
The small terracotta was
made when Canova was
only eighteen years old,
and established himself
as the last great exponent
of eighteenth-century
Venetian figurative culture.

16

Antonio Canova
(Possagno 1757–Venice 1822)
15. *Apollo*
Terracotta, 61 × 17 cm
Cat. 550
Acquisition: 1807,
from the old Accademia
Latest restoration: 1987

This is probably the
preparatory model for
the sculpture on the same
subject, as a pendant to the
Daphne, commissioned by
the Procurator of San Marco
Ludovico Rezzonico, which
was left unfinished in 1779,
before Canova's departure for
Rome, and then destroyed.
The signature is traced
with a brush on the base.
With this sculpture, today
mutilated, Antonio Canova
accompanied his application
of March 30, 1779, to become
a member of the Academy,
to which he was elected
unanimously on April 5,
1779. In this superb
terracotta model, the young
artist shows he is aware of
the art of Bernini, despite his
eighteenth-century training.
Several sketches by Bernini
were present in the Farsetti
collection, which Canova
studied assiduously.

Antonio Canova
(Possagno 1757–Venice 1822)
16. *Pietà*
Clay, 21 × 34 cm
Cat. 552
Acquisition: 1911,
by purchase
Latest restoration: 1980

The signature is engraved
on the base at the center.
After Canova died, this
work was passed down to his
student Baruzzi who donated
it in 1831 to the clergyman
Gardenghi. Gardenghi's
brother gave it to Cardinal
Baruffi, the Bishop of Imola,
who then left it to his heirs.
A late work based on
a common subject, it
nonetheless maintains
the quick spirit of invention
found in the artist's earlier
works.

15

19 Boccaccio Boccaccino, Bartolomeo Montagna and Giovanni Agostino da Lodi

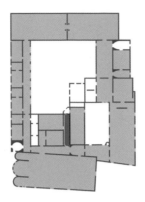

This is a corridor which connects with Rooms 20 and 21, showing fifteenth-century "Story" cycles. The platform at the back with the sash window, from which one can admire the view of the Palladio convent, was designed by Carlo Scarpa in 1947.

Giovanni Agostino da Lodi
Washing of the Feet, detail.

Giovanni Agostino da Lodi
(active from ca. 1490–
recorded until ca. 1520)
1. *Washing of the Feet*
Panel, 132 × 111 cm
Cat. 599
Acquisition: 1856, purchase
from the Manfrin collection
Latest restoration: 1991–92

The date of 1500 is painted
on Saint Peter's stool.
The work is inspired
by the arrangement
of the heads and the
physical characterizations
of the *Last Supper*
by Leonardo da Vinci,
and there are also numerous
references to Bramantino.
The original location
of the work is unknown,
but it was probably made
for Venice since it is well
known and was often
imitated there.

1

2

3

184

4

Pietro de Saliba (?)
(Messina, active from
the late fifteenth century–
early sixteenth century)
2. *Christ at the Column*
Panel, 40 × 33 cm
Cat. 589
Acquisition: 1856,
by purchase from
the Manfrin collection
Latest restoration: 1993

This painting was part
of a group of works depicting
the bust of Christ crowned
with thorns and against
a column with a rope around
his neck; the works were
all based on a model by
Antonello which may be his
Christ, now at the Louvre.

Antonello de Saliba
(Messina ca. 1467–ca. 1535)
3. *The Virgin Annunciate*
Panel, 47 × 34 cm
Cat. 590
Acquisition: 1812,
following the suppressions
Latest restoration: 1993

Originally in the Sala
dell'Anticollegio at the Doge's
Palace, the work was part
of a group of paintings
donated to the Republic
by Bertucci Contarini.
Although it was long believed
to be the work of Antonello
da Messina, it is instead
a copy of the *Virgin
Annunciate* by the master
in the Galleria Nazionale
in Palermo, completed
around 1476–77. The
presence of Venetian motifs
derived from Bellini and
Montagna confirmed that
the piece was by Antonello
de Saliba (the son of a
brother-in-law of Antonello
da Messina), who resided
in Venice from 1480 to 1497,
when he is, in fact,
unrecorded in Messina.

Marco Basaiti, attr.
(Venice 1470/75–after 1530)
4. *Saint Jerome*
Panel, 54 × 42 cm
Cat. 107
Acquisition: 1816, by bequest
from Girolamo Molin
Latest restoration: 1993

A work for private devotion,
the subject was copied many
times by Basaiti; this may be
from the artist's later period.

Marco Basaiti, attr.
(Venice 1470/75–after 1530)
5. *Christ between Two Angels*
Panel, 39 × 103 cm
Cat. 108
Acquisition: 1812–14,
following the suppressions
Latest restoration: 1993

This piece came to the
Accademia Galleries together
with *Saint James the Apostle*
and *Saint Anthony the Abbot*
(Room 19, cats. 68/A, 68)
from the convent of Santa
Maria dei Miracoli. It is
traditionally attributed to
Basaiti, and the most recent
restoration revealed its
outstandingly high quality.
The representation of
Christ's dead body—typical of
Venetian painters—is deeply
rooted in Byzantine
iconography. Similarities are
also in evidence between this
work and Carpaccio's
Mourning of the Dead Christ
at the Staatliche Museen
of Berlin.

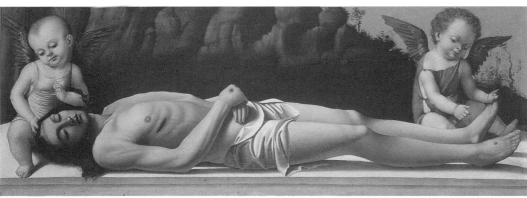

5

Room 19

6

Bartolomeo Cincani known as Bartolomeo Montagna
(Vicenza ca. 1449–1523)
6. *Saint Peter Blessing and Devotee*
Panel, 60 × 39 cm
Cat. 1343
Acquisition: 1971,
by purchase
Latest restoration: 1979

On the scroll held in the mouth of the dog is written "esto fidelis" (be faithful). Because of its affinity with the frescoes in the Verona church of Santi Nazaro e Celso, the work has been attributed to Montagna since 1871, when it was recorded in the Papafava collection in Padua. The painting dates to around 1505. The work reveals the artist's particular ability to bring together the human figure, architecture and landscape. The influence of Antonello da Messina is enriched with aspects inspired by Giovanni Bellini, especially evident in the enchanting background of the Veneto mainland: among the various buildings one can recognize the façade of the Duomo of Vicenza and the Arena of Pola.

Jacopo Parisati known as Jacopo da Montagnana
(recorded from 1458–Padua 1499)
7. *The Angel of the Annunciation*
8. *The Virgin Annunciate*
Panels, 185 × 74 cm, 185 × 76 cm
Cats. 606, 608
Acquisition: 1812,
following the suppressions
Latest restoration: 1984

Originally in the church of Monteortone (Padua), these panels must once have formed a single painting. A central part measuring about 110 centimeters appears to have been cut out, evident also from the interruption of the bed with the red canopy. Vasari (1550) also notes that "il Montagnana [...] fece in Padova a Santa Maria di Monte Artone una tavola nella chiesa" ("Montagnana [...] painted a panel in the church of Santa Maria di Monteortone in Padua"). The work, which was completed between 1494 and 1497, represents the artist's translation of the teachings of Mantegna into a more refined decorativism.

7

8

9

Boccaccio Boccaccino
(Ferrara? before August 2,
1466–Cremona ca. 1524/25)
9. *Mystic Marriage of Saint
Catherine with Saints Rose,
Peter and John the Baptist,
the Announcement
to the Shepherds, the Flight
into Egypt and the Magi
on Horseback*
Panel, 87 × 143 cm
Cat 600
Acquisition: 1838, by
donation from Girolamo
Contarini
Latest restoration: 1993

The signature is at the lower
right. The work was
completed at the end of the
artist's stay in Venice (1506),
with many elements taken
from Bellini, Carpaccio and
Giorgione, and even some
echoes of the *Madonna
of the Rosary* by Dürer,
displayed in 1506 in the
church of San Bartolomeo.

Marco Basaiti
(Venice 1470/75–post 1530)
10. *Saint James the Apostle*
11. *Saint Anthony the Abbot*
Panels, 114 × 35 cm each
Cats. 68/A, 68
Acquisition: 1812–14,
following the suppressions
Latest restoration: 1993

The two panels signed
"Marcus and Basait. p."
(Marco Basaiti painted)
on their respective
pedestals appear to be
of different quality, but still
similar in style to Marco
d'Oggiono, who was called
on to make some paintings
for the Milanesi confraternity
at the Frari in 1497 and
1498, for whom Basaiti
was also completing
the large altar-piece
of Saint Ambrose after
the death of Alvise Vivarini.

10

11

12

Marco Marziale
(recorded from 1493 to 1507)
12. *Supper at Emmaus*
Panel, 122 × 141 cm
Cat. 76
Acquisition: 1838,
by donation from
Girolamo Contarini
Latest restoration: 1993

The signature and date
(1506) are on a scroll
on the leg of the table.
The iconographic source
of the subject, with its

Dürer-inspired details,
must have been the lost
Supper at Emmaus by
Giovanni Bellini mentioned
by Vasari (1568) in the
Giorgio Cornaro collection,
known now from the
engraving made of it by
Pietro Monaco and the copy
(made with collaborators) in
the church of San Salvador.
Another variation was
painted by Marziale in 1507,
now at the Staatliche Museen
of Berlin.

13

Vittore Carpaccio
(Venice ca. 1460–
before June 1526)
13. *Apparition of the
Crucifixes of Mount Ararat
in the Church of
Sant'Antonio in Castello*
Canvas, 121 × 174 cm
Cat. 91
Acquisition: 1838,
from the warehouse
of Commenda following
the suppressions
Latest restoration: 2005

Originally in the church
of Sant'Antonio in Castello,
the work depicts the vision
seen by Francesco Ottoboni,
the prior of the convent,
when he invoked the aid
of the Martyrs of Mount
Ararat during a plague in
1511. The Martyrs appeared
to him in a dream entering
in a procession into the
church led by Saint Peter.
The interior, with the
wooden "barco" (a structure
similar to a chancel),

the ex voto, the altar
and the polyptychs offers
us an interesting image
of a Venetian church
at the beginning of the
1500s—still Gothic in style,
but undergoing remodeling.
The work is fascinating for
its important historical
and documentary value.
Its recent restoration has
confirmed the attribution
to Carpaccio (Boschini 1664).
To the left, the Ottoboni altar
is represented, where the

great altarpiece of the
*Crucifixion and the
Apotheosis of the 10,000
Martyrs of Mount Ararat*
(Room 2, cat. 89) by the
same painter would be
mounted. Datable to
ca. 1512–13.

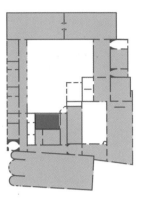

This room was already constructed in 1940. Seven years later the canvases with the *Miracles of the Cross* were placed here provisionally; in 1959–60 Carlo Scarpa completed the arrangement, which has remained practically unchanged ever since. The cycle originally served to adorn the walls of the Albergo Room or the Cross Room in the Scuola di San Giovanni Evangelista, where there is still a relic of the Holy Cross on display, donated to the guild in 1369 by Filippo de Mezières, the Great Chancellor of the kingdom of Cyprus. There were originally nine canvases, including the *Miracle of the Vendramin Ships*

by Pietro Perugino, completed in 1494. Unfortunately only eight are on display at the Accademia; Perugino's canvas—composed while he was in Venice working in the Doge's Palace—was destroyed and replaced in 1588. The most detailed record on these canvases is a pamphlet from 1590 which describes the *Miracles*, supplying the artist's name and year of completion of the paintings. The Scuola di San Giovanni Evangelista was suppressed by Napoleonic decree in 1806, and the works were delivered to the Accademia in 1820; they were displayed separately at various times until they were finally brought back together in 1947.

Vittore Carpaccio
Miracle of the Relic of the True Cross on the Rialto Bridge, detail.

1

Vittore Carpaccio
(Venice ca. 1460–
before June 1526)
1. *Miracle of the Relic
of the True Cross
on the Rialto Bridge*
(*The Healing of the Possessed
Man*)
Canvas, 371 × 392 cm
Cat. 566
Acquisition: 1820,
following the suppressions
Latest restoration: 1990–91

This canvas was completed
in 1494 for the east wall
of the Albergo to the right
of the altar, and narrates
the miraculous healing
of a possessed man.
The work was obtained
by Francesco Querini—the
patriarch of Grado—through
the reliquary of the Sacred
Cross. In 1544, after hearing
the opinion of "prudente

messer Tizian pictor"
("the sagacious painter
Titian"), a part was cut at the
bottom left near the opening
of the door which led to the
"Albergo Nuovo," built during
this period. The gap was
then arbitrarily integrated.
The artist synthesizes three
fundamental moments:
the procession on the bridge,
the entrance of the patriarch,
and the miracle which takes
place on the loggia. But even
this event is overshadowed
by the representation of the
city itself. The bridge is still
the wooden one constructed
in 1458, with the drawbridge
open at the center to allow
larger boats to pass. This
collapsed in 1524, and was
replaced by the present one
made of stone. On the left
can be seen the emblem of
the Albergo dello Storione

and the loggia, where the
market's patrons would
gather. On the right, the
Fondaco dei Tedeschi,
destroyed by fire in 1505,
Ca' da Mosto with its portico
which still exists today, the
campanile of San Giovanni
Crisostomo and the one of
Santi Apostoli, rebuilt in 1672.
The contrast with the analytic
realism of the other canvases
further reveals Carpaccio's
descriptive abilities and his
emphasis on chromatics.

Giovanni Mansueti
(recorded in Venice
from 1485–died between
September 1526 and
March 1527)
2. *The Miraculous Healing
of the Daughter of
Benvegnudo of San Polo*
Canvas, 361 × 299 cm
Cat. 562

Acquisition: 1820,
following the suppressions
Latest restoration: 1990

This work illustrates the
miraculous event that took
place in 1414, when the
daughter of Benvegnudo,
who had been immobile
since birth, was miraculously
healed when touched by
three candles that her father
had placed near the relic.
Completed after 1502, this
canvas has great historical
interest, and recalls
techniques employed
by Carpaccio in his Saint
Ursula cycle (Room 21),
but also imitated by other
artists, such as Paolo
Veronese, who will mimic the
"dead stairs" and the arcades
framing the narration in his
Feast in the House of Levi
(Room 10, cat. 203).

Gentile Bellini
(Venice 1429–1507)
3. *Miracle of the Relic of the Cross on San Lorenzo Bridge*
Canvas, 326 × 435 cm
Cat. 568
Acquisition: 1820,
following the suppressions
Latest restoration: 1989–90

At the center are the signature and date (1500). According to legend, between 1370 and 1382, during a procession to the church of San Lorenzo, the relic accidentally fell into the canal, and only the Great Guardian Andrea Vendramin could grab it. The painting is also interesting for its depiction of the urban scene.
To the left Caterina Cornaro and her ladies witness the scene, while the five people kneeling to the right have been identified as members of the painter's family, but it is more likely that they are high ranking members of the Scuola.

2

3

4

Gentile Bellini
(Venice 1429–1507)
4. *Miraculous Healing
of Pietro de' Ludovici*
Canvas, 368 × 263 cm
Cat. 563
Acquisition: 1820,
following the suppressions
Latest restoration: 1992

The signature—not the
original—is on an inscription
on the steps, repeating
an ancient tradition.
It is unclear if the graft
on the lower part of the
work—rather rough and
repainted—was in relation
to the placement of a
doorway. The work depicts
how Pietro de' Ludovici
was healed of his quartan
fever after touching a candle
that had been near the
relic of the saint he was
worshipping. The painting
was probably completed
in 1501 using drawings
by Gentile's father Jacopo,
and with extensive graphic
work by Gentile himself.

5

Gentile Bellini
(Venice 1429–1507)
5. *Procession in Piazza San Marco*
Canvas, 373 × 745 cm
Cat. 567
Acquisition: 1820, following the suppressions
Latest restoration: 1988–89

At the bottom in the center of the painting can be read the artist's signature and the date, 1496. Two large grafts at the ends of the lower part probably correspond to two doorways on the front wall of the altar (Ridolfi 1648); they were filled when the painting was moved to opposite the windows after the seventeenth-century remodeling project by Massari. The first of Gentile's paintings for the cycle, it depicts the procession taking place in Saint Mark's Square on the Feast of Saint Mark. All the Scuole participated in this affair with their respective relics. In particular, the event that took place on April 25, 1444, when the Brescian merchant Jacopo de' Salis prayed for and received help for his gravely wounded son. But this miracle is described with less attention than the square itself, which is shown here as it appeared before the changes made to it in the sixteenth century. The Basilica still glistens with its original mosaics, of which only one exists today. The arches and the Porta della Carta (the main door) radiate with gold and various colors. To the right, next to the ancient campanile, appears the Orseolo Hospice, demolished about fifty years later when Sansovino redesigned the square, here still with its pink brick paving and built the Procuratie Nuove.

Room 20

6

Benedetto Rusconi known as Benedetto Diana
(Venice ca. 1460–1525)
6. *Miracle of the Relic of the Holy Cross*
Canvas, 371 × 150 cm
Cat. 565
Acquisition: 1820, following the suppressions
Latest restoration: 1990

This painting depicts an episode that took place on March 10, 1480, when the son of Ser Alvise Finetti was healed after falling from a loft. The work reveals the influence of the most advanced artists of the time, especially Giorgione and Lotto, and was probably completed by 1510.

Lazzaro Bastiani
(Venice ca. 1425/30–1512)
7. *Offering of the Relic of the Cross to the Members of the Scuola Grande di San Giovanni Evangelista*
Canvas, 324 × 441 cm
Cat. 561
Acquisition: 1820, following the suppressions
Latest restoration: 1992

The painting shows Filippo de Mezières offering the miraculous relic. The episode is depicted from the exterior, and provides a valuable testimony of buildings which were later modified or destroyed. We can recognize the old façade of the church of San Giovanni Evangelista with its portico which was later demolished. To the left on the side of the Scuola can be seen the circular windows—the existence of which recent restoration projects have also confirmed—and the raising of the large hall by about 2 meters, which occurred in 1495. In this same year, according to the 1590 pamphlet, Bastiani painted this work, probably immediately after the alterations.

Giovanni Mansueti
(recorded in Venice from 1485–died between September 1526 and March 1527)
8. *Miracle of the Relic of the Cross in Campo San Lio*
Canvas, 322 × 463 cm
Cat. 564
Acquisition: 1820, following the suppressions
Latest restoration: 1990

On the inscription held by the person on the left bringing a hand towards his hat—probably a self-portrait—can be read the signature of the painter, who considered himself a disciple of Bellini. The remarkable event occurred in 1474 during the funeral of a member of the confraternity who had not had enough faith in the relic; the cross became incredibly heavy and had to be entrusted to the parish priest of San Lio. Probably painted in 1494, Mansueti must have used a preparatory drawing by Gentile Bellini, now in the Uffizi. The writing on the scroll at the far right of the side of the church is curious: "Casa da fitar ducati 5" ("House for rent, 5 ducats").

7

8

21 Vittore Carpaccio's
Legend of Saint Ursula

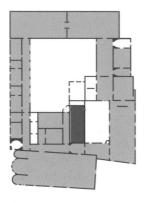

In this room, which once held the collection of Girolamo Contarini, the *Legend of Saint Ursula* cycle by Carpaccio was installed between 1921 and 1923. From 1959–60 Carlo Scarpa remodeled the room, lowering the paintings, which he supported and surrounded by a strip of light oak with a thin gilt border. The altarpiece, set slightly back and illuminated from the side by a new source of light, was separated from the canvases by wooden screens. The paintings used to decorate the walls of the Scuola di Sant'Orsola, a religious confraternity founded in the fourteenth century at the basilica of Santi Giovanni e Paolo. Many Venetian aristocrats belonged to the confraternity, including the Loredan family as well as numerous members of the Compagnia della Calza ("Company of the Stocking"), a sort of club set up by young men, most of them from the nobility, who chose to combine their forces in order to amuse themselves and wore stockings quartered in different colors or magnificently embroidered as an emblem. The pictorial decoration represents the story of Ursula, one of the stock of legends of medieval Europe collected in the thirteenth century by the Dominican Jacobus da Varagine in a compendium called the *Legenda Aurea*. Various compilations were published, culminating in Nicola de' Minerbi's Venetian edition of 1475. Carpaccio draws freely on this source, embellishing it with references to dogal ceremonies, theatrical performances and contemporary festivals and weaving it together with the story of Giulgelma, daughter of the king of England and bride of the king of Hungary. The dates on the giant canvases range from 1490 to 1495, but their execution must have taken several years longer, at least as far as the "Embassies" are concerned, given that the clock of St. Mark's, not inaugurated until February 1, 1499, appears in the *Arrival of the Ambassadors*. With the suppressions the works were transferred to the Accademia Galleries, where they can be seen today in their original sequence, while the Scuola, whose outer walls are still visible on the exterior, was later incorporated into the house of the canons of Santi Giovanni e Paolo.

Vittore Carpaccio
The Arrival of the English Ambassadors, detail.

Vittore Carpaccio
(Venice ca. 1460–
before June 1526)
1. *Arrival of the English
Ambassadors*
Canvas, 278 × 589 cm
Cat. 572
Acquisition: 1812,
following the suppressions
Latest restoration: 1983

At the lower center
is the inscription:
"op. victoris / carpatio/ veneti."
The works do not observe the
logical sequence of the story,
which actually begins

with this canvas. The piece
condenses three scenes,
set off by three architectural
elements: the arrival
of the ambassadors
at the court of Brittany
and the presentation
of Prince Ethereus's marriage
proposal; Ursula in her
room relates to her father
the marriage conditions
she requires while the nurse
waits at the foot of the stairs.
She, like the young man
in a red toga at the far left,
frames the episode of the
embassies, which together

with the next two canvases
covered an entire wall of the
Scuola, introducing a long
"secular" lead-up to the
religious core of the story.
In fact the luxurious
surroundings of the courts
of Brittany and Anglia were
suitable settings for portraits
of the members of the
confraternity and able
to satisfy their desire to
celebrate their own status.
As on the canvas with the
*Meeting and Departure
of the Betrothed* (Room 21,
cat 575), at the center is a

person with the emblem on
his sleeve of the Compagnia
della Calza degli Ortolani,
a guild of pleasure-seeking
nobles.
The canvas, painted as
a sacred representation
or a theatrical scene, has
a piece missing in the lower
part, where a door had been
opened very early on.
On this occasion, the face
of a page boy on the right
was probably overpainted.
It came to light in the recent
restoration, but the rest
of the figure is irrecoverable.

1

The building in the center
is inspired by the Temple of
Jerusalem, from xylographies
by Reeuwich (1486), while
the influence of Perugino,
who was in Venice in 1494,
is evident in the arches
to the left. Preparatory
drawings are kept at Christ
Church Library in Oxford,
the National Museum
of Fine Arts in Valletta, the
British Museum in London
and the Nationalmuseet
in Stockholm.

Room 21

2

Vittore Carpaccio
(Venice ca. 1460–
before June 1526)
2. *Dismissal
of the Ambassadors*
Canvas, 281 × 252 cm
Cat. 573
Acquisition: 1812,
following the suppressions
Latest restoration: 1984

At the bottom left
on the scroll the inscription
reads: "victoris car / ...
veneti / opus." In the
extraordinary interior
in the style of the
Lombardos, a splendid
example of "the science
of perspective and skillful
coloring," Ursula's father
concludes the negotiations
and gives the ambassadors
his reply for the king
of England. It is one
of the most complex canvases
in the cycle, in which
a calculated abstraction
and an equally deliberate
absence of analysis of the
figures' features tend to lend
emphasis to the space
and the architecture.
The cutaway of the grand
hall, with its inlaid marbles,
recalls the contemporary
architecture of Codussi and
Pietro and Tullio Lombardo.
The ceremony, inspired
by the ones held in the
Doge's Palace, is recorded
by the scrivener on the right,
who thus takes on the role
of chronicler. The interest
in space and neglect
of portraiture suggests that
the canvas was not painted
at the time of the other
two embassies but closer
to the *Dream of Ursula*,
dated 1495.

3

Vittore Carpaccio
(Venice ca. 1460–
before June 1526)
3. Return of the Ambassadors
Canvas, 297 × 526 cm
Cat. 574
Acquisition: 1812,
following the suppressions
Latest restoration: 1983

At the lower left is the
inscription: "victoris / ca ...
tio / veneti / opus," and
on the base of the pennant
is an indication of a
restoration in 1623.
The last of the negotiations:
the return home of the

English messengers with
Ursula's reply is announced
near a pier by a small
page boy and by a "steward,"
whose job it was to
introduce the ambassadors
to the Doge's banquet to the
accompaniment of musicians.
The ceremony is thus taken
from the one in use in the
Venetian Republic. Here,
history and news overlap,
evidenced by the young
English messenger advancing
to the left with the insignia
of the Venetian Compagnia
della Calza society. The young
man viewed from behind

who seems to mark the ideal
center of the composition
may be Prince Ethereus
himself, come down
to meet the ambassadors.
The story unfolds in
an urban setting that,
while it is not Venice,
offers constant reminders
of it (such as the two
towers on the left,
resembling those of the
arsenal), following a logic
that would become typical
of the eighteenth-century
capriccio.

Room 21

4

Vittore Carpaccio
(Venice ca. 1460–
before June 1526)
4. *Meeting and Departure
of the Betrothed*
Canvas, 279 × 610 cm
Cat. 575
Acquisition: 1812,
following the suppressions
Latest restoration: 1983–84

At the base of the pennant
on an inscription are
the signature and date:
"victoris / carpatio /

veneti-opus / MCCCCLXXXXV."
This canvas is divided into
three episodes: the prince
takes leave of his parents
before departing; the
betrothed couple bid farewell
to the king and queen, and
finally they set sail on the
ships which will bring them
to Rome. In the background
are shown the locations
of the story: on the left
is medieval England, while
on the right is Renaissance
Brittany, with the tower

of the Knights of Rhodes
and the tower of Saint Mark
in Crete, taken from
woodcuts by Reeuwich
(1486). These buildings
would seem to confirm
the hypothesis that the story
of Ursula alludes to that
of Caterina Cornaro, the
queen of Cyprus. The two
youths at the center are
members of the Compagnia
della Calza. The seated
one has the emblem of the
Ortolani or the Zardinieri

on his sleeve, and the initials
"F.Z." (Fratres Zardinieri),
and on a legging the initials
"S.A." (Societas Amicorum).
The standing one holds
a scroll on which can be read
the letters: "n.l.d.d.v.v.g.v.i.,"
which stand for "nicolaus
laurentanus donum dedit
ursulae virginis gloriosa
virginibusque inclitis."
It is thus likely that the
commissioner—at least
of this work—was Nicolò
Loredan (Gentili 1996).

5

Vittore Carpaccio
(Venice ca. 1460–
before June 1526)
5. The Dream of Saint Ursula
Canvas, 273 × 267 cm
Cat. 578
Acquisition: 1812,
following the suppressions
Latest restoration: 1984

On the inscription at the foot
of the bed is the apocryphal
inscription, but which
surely respects the
original version: "victor carp /
f / MCCCCLXXXXV."
This is the most damaged
canvas, so much so that it

was only exhibited in 1852
in order to ensure the unity
of the cycle. Here Ursula
receives the announcement
of martyrdom from an angel
while she sleeps in her room.
This work reveals a strong
Flemish influence, with
one of the most suggestive
interiors of Renaissance
painting. The light shed
by the dawn shows all
the objects in the room,
laden with symbolic
significance, such as
the myrtle and clove plants
on the biforate window
which allude to conjugal love

and faithfulness. On the base
of the statue of Hercules
above the door is the
inscription "diva f.av./st.a"
(divine announcements
are propitious), indicating
that the prophesy is actually
favorable, in spite of its
apparent dramatic nature.
A beautiful preparatory
drawing is at the Uffizi
in Florence, and shows
an additional two biforate
windows in the back wall.

6

Vittore Carpaccio
(Venice ca. 1460–
before June 1526)
6. *The Pilgrims Meet Pope
Cyriac*
Canvas, 279 × 305 cm
Cat. 577
Acquisition: 1812,
following the suppressions
Latest restoration: 1984

On the scroll is the
inscription: "victoris car /
patio veneti / opus." After
a long voyage, the pilgrims
have reached the gates
of Rome where they meet
Pope Cyriac before the

Castel Sant'Angelo, in
accordance with an old
diplomatic tradition
"for important visitors
arriving on the Via Aurelia"
(Zorzi 1988). The pontefice
decides to join the royal
entourage after the baptism
of Ethereus and the
coronation of the couple.
The ceremony replicates
a Doge's procession,
as indicated by the
umbrella—a typical attribute
of the highest city authorities
of Venice.
Carpaccio was probably
influenced by a Giovanni

Bellini painting from the
lost cycle with the stories
of Alexander III in the Doge's
Palace. The figure in the red
toga to the right
of the pope—a "didascalos,"
someone who would
point out the more salient
elements in plays—has been
identified as the Venetian
humanist Ermolao Barbaro,
who died in the Republic's
disfavor in 1493; this fact
makes it unlikely that
the artist would portray
him before that date.

7

Vittore Carpaccio
(Venice ca. 1460–before June
1526)
7. *Arrival in Cologne*
Canvas, 279 × 254 cm
Cat. 579
Acquisition: 1812,
following the suppressions
Latest restoration: 1984

To the lower left on a scroll
is the inscription: "op. victoris
/ charpatio / veneti-
MCCCCLXXXX.M / septembris."
This is surely the first painting
made by the artist, evident not
only because of the date, but
also because of the apparent
difficulty in articulating the
simultaneous representation of
many subjects in the available
space. It was probably made
smaller—especially at the
right, where the gates of
Cologne were entirely visible,
as in the print by Giovanni del
Pian (1785). The pilgrim's ships
are shown with Ursula and
the Pope distinguishable
on the first, as they arrive
in Cologne to find that the city
is under siege by the Huns.
In the foreground a warrior
reads the message sent by
some traitorous Roman princes
warning the barbarians of their
arrival. The effect of the gallery
that dominates the scene,
a typical merchant transport
ship, is truly exceptional.
The scene is taken from
an engraving in the *Filocolo*
by Boccaccio in the Neapolitan
edition of 1475, confirmation
of Carpaccio's vast knowledge
of the illustrated books in his
possession, and of his original
ability to transpose the images.

8

Vittore Carpaccio
(Venice ca. 1460–
before June 1526)
8. *Martyrdom of the Pilgrims
and the Funeral of Ursula*
Canvas, 271 × 560 cm
Cat. 580
Acquisition: 1812,
following the suppressions
Latest restoration: 1984

On the base of the column
is the inscription with the
date and the signature:
"victoris / carpatio / veneti-
opus / MCCCCLXXX/XIII."
The column divides the two
moments of the event, and
carries on it the coat of arms
of the Loredan family, who
commissioned the work.
On the left the massacre
of the pilgrims, culminating
with the killing of the Pope
and Ursula, who is about
to be slain by an archer.
A warrior witnesses the
scene, powerless to help; he
may be the Hun prince Julio
who, according to legend,
had tried in vain to save
the princess. On the right
the funeral of the martyrs
takes place in a mausoleum
bearing the inscription
"ursula." The veiled woman
kneeling at the foot of the
catafalque could be based
on Orsa (Orsola), the wife
of Antonio Loredan, the
hero of Scutari. It is also
probable that the slaughter
of the pilgrims referred
to the massacres of Christian
men and women perpetrated
by the Turks.

Vittore Carpaccio
(Venice ca. 1460–
before June 1526)
9. *Apotheosis of Saint Ursula*
Canvas, 481 × 335 cm
Cat. 576
Acquisition: 1812,
following the suppressions
Latest restoration: 1982–83

At the lower center
on the notice is written the
date: "op. victoris / carpatio /
MCCCCLXXXXI."
The altarpiece shows
the apotheosis of Ursula,
supported by a sheaf

of palms held by a double
crown of seraphs and flanked
by two crossed standards.
She is received in heaven
by the Eternal Father who
bestows the celestial crown
upon her. Her companions,
participants in the event,
observe the scene, and
to the left are three male
figures who could be
Giovanni, Marco and Jacopo,
sons of Antonio Loredan.
In the background, the
walled and turreted city
is evidently Cologne, while
to the right on top of the

mountain next to the lake
is Scutari, defended
against the Turks by
Antonio Loredan himself.
The ascension of Ursula is
similar to an "Assumption of
the Virgin," and particularly
to Mantegna's *Assumption* in
the Ovetari Chapel in Padua.
For this work, as for the 1510
altarpiece for the church
of San Giobbe (Room 2,
cat. 44), Carpaccio used
two splendid preparatory
drawings inspired by
Perugino now kept in the
Ashmolean Museum, Oxford.

9

22 Neoclassical Anteroom

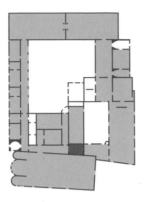

The arrangement of this small circular room
that leads into the Sala dell'Albergo was
overseen by Francesco Lazzari between 1821
and 1823, who decorated it with sculptures
and bas-reliefs by Canova-influenced artists.

Jacopo De Martini
Hector Scolds Paris, detail.

1

4

Rinaldo Rinaldi
(Padua 1793–Rome 1873)
1. *Adonis*
Marble, height 153 cm
Cat. S 26
Latest restoration: 1983

On the base to the left
the date, 1816, is engraved.
A neoclassical work, the
pendant of the statue
of the same subject
in the niche in front of it.

Rinaldo Rinaldi
(Padua 1793–Rome 1873)
2. *Hector Bids Farewell
to Andromache*
Bas-relief, plaster,
81 × 147 cm
Cat. S 223
Acquisition: 1813–14, trial
work for second year in Rome
Latest restoration: 1983

Rinaldi, who was a student
at the Venice Accademia,
won the Rome "pensionato"
scholarship competition
in April 1812. This bas-relief
is the trial work sent to
Venice for his second year
of study, as required by the
regulations.

Antonio Giaccarelli
(Venice 1739–Milan 1838)
3. *Priam Asks Achilles
for the Body of Hector*
Bas-relief, plaster,
96 × 180 cm
Cat. S 231
Latest restoration: 1983

Made by the artist when
he was still a student
at the Accademia between
1819 and around 1825.

Jacopo De Martini
(Venice 1793–1841)
4. *Adonis*
Marble, height, 158 cm
Cat. S 30
Latest restoration: 1983

An academic representation
of the neoclassical standards
of beauty.
This is a pendant of the
statue in the facing niche.

2

3

Room 22

5

6

Jacopo De Martini
(Venice 1793–1841)
5. *Hector Scolds Paris*
Bas-relief, plaster,
90 × 180 cm
Cat. S 226
Acquisition: 1816–17,
trial work for second year
in Rome
Latest restoration: 1983

De Martini won the
competition for an
apprenticeship in Rome in
1815. Due to health problems

it was difficult for him
to attend, and he withdrew in
1818, before completing the
training. The work
was sent by him to the
Accademia during his second
year of study, as required
by the regulations.

Jacopo De Martini
(Venice 1793–1841)
6. *Enone Refuses to Assist
the Wounded Paris*
Bas-relief, plaster,
90 × 156 cm
Cat. S 227
Acquisition: 1816–17
Latest restoration: 1983

Reveals its Canovian
derivation in the female
figures, despite the extremely
emphatic gestures.

Jacopo De Martini
(Venezia 1793–1841)
7. *Rape of Ganymede*
Plaster, 88 × 103 × 26 cm
Cat. S 225

The sculpture is a faithful
copy of the famous Roman
marble of the second century
AD, part of the collection of
Giovanni Grimani, formerly
displayed in the Statuario
della Serenissima and now
in the Tribune of the Palazzo
Grimani in Venice.

7

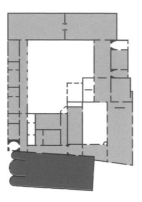

The founding of the church of Santa Maria della Carità, which probably occurred at the beginning of the twelfth century, is part history, part myth. According to Sansovino (1581), it was originally a small wooden building "... around a capital of an image of the Virgin, famous for various miracles." Only later was it decided to construct a church in stone on the site. In 1134 some Augustinian monks from Santa Maria in Porto relocated from Ravenna to Venice and built their convent next to the church of Santa Maria della Carità. According to legend, in 1177 Pope Alexander III—in order to escape from Frederick Barbarossa—hid in the convent for six months and consecrated the church on April 5. From then on, every year on that date the Doge and Venetians of every class—even the inhabitants of the provinces—came to the church of Santa Maria della Carità to obtain the papal indulgence he had granted for the help received. Crossing the Grand Canal to the church was made easier by the construction of a bridge of boats from Campo San Vidal to Campo Santa Maria della Carità. This custom lasted until the end of the Republic. The old façade of the church can be seen in a painting kept in Room 24, which illustrates the meeting of the Doge and the Pope. From archival documents we know that at the end of the thirteenth century the church had an external portico—once very common on Venetian buildings—of which there are now only two examples remaining: one at San Giacomo di Rialto and another at San Nicolò dei Mendicoli. There was also a bell tower for this original structure, which was left intact even during the modifications made in the fifteenth century, until on March 17, 1744, when, due to the erosion at its base, it finally succumbed and toppled into the Grand Canal. There were many illustrious figures buried there as we can deduce from the register published by Tassini in 1876; a part of this register still exists in the Seminary. The ascension of Gabriele

Condulmer from the order of the Lateran Canons to the papacy (Eugene IV) in 1431, and his long pontificate, which lasted until 1447, brought new-found glory and power to the monks of the Carità. In fact, after prolonged negotiations with the members of the Scuola di Santa Maria della Carità, the monks obtained approval to enlarge the church. The new construction began in April of 1441 and was overseen by Bartolomeo Bon. Working with his son, Giovanni, Bon was responsible for all the stonework that carried the new structure: the windows, the door with the lunette above it, the side door, the round eye which was once part of the façade, the statues of Saint Augustine, Saint Jerome and the Holy Father, the small bell towers, the pinnacles, the leaves on the spire of the façade (most of which now lost), the side pillars, the ribs for the archivolts of the chapels, the cantilevers and every other decoration. At the same time, the walls were constructed in brick up to the roof, supported by fifteen enormous beams from the region of Cadore, today still resting upon Bon's cantilevers which were completed in May of 1446, with the monogram "Ihesus." In 1450 the apse chapels were built and alongside Bartolomeo Bon we still find "Maestro Pantaleon," who appears to have been associated with Bon in many important workshops in Venice at that time, including the one at Ca' d'Oro. The decoration painted with large leaves which runs under the scarp wall of the roof and surrounds the eye on all the windows was the work of Ercole, the son of Jacobello del Fiore, who, in June of 1449, received fifty ducats for each work "... done in the Carità" and twelve more ducats in December of 1453 for the decoration of the chapels. Once the construction was completed, the friars decorated it with precious works of art spending 60 ducats for a large crucifix; in 1451 another 68 ducats were paid to Petrus Christus for importing an altarpiece, which increased up to 100 ducats once transport and customs expenses were added. In 1453 a *Madonna* was bought from Donatello, who was sojourning in Padua

at the time; the painting was placed over the door of the sacristy. Other works were commissioned from Jacopo, Gentile and Giovanni Bellini and their workshop and from Cima da Conegliano. Many important funereal monuments were also erected, such as the one for the doges Marco and Agostino Barbarigo. Parts of these statues remain today and are preserved in the Franchetti Gallery at Ca' d'Oro and in the Seminary. In 1807, the whole complex of the Carità—comprising the convent, church and school—was chosen to be the site of an Academy of Fine Arts and an accompanying gallery. Begun in 1811, the modifications were headed by the architect Giannantonio Selva. The church was completely overhauled: every decoration was removed, the "barco" (a structure similar to a chancel) and the chapels were destroyed, the Gothic windows were walled over and the entire space was divided horizontally to create five large rooms on the upper floor, lit by skylights for exhibiting. The bas-relief work by Bartolomeo Bon on the façade showing the *Coronation of the Virgin* was removed, and is now preserved in the old sacristy of the church of the Salute. From 1921 to 1923, under the direction of Gino Fogolari and with the architect Aldo Scolari, the whole space with the apses was restored including the truss ceiling and the Gothic windows on the side walls. In 1948 the room was remodeled by Carlo Scarpa. He removed from the walls some broad replicas which were to imitate the original wall decoration, and placed the paintings on large larch panels lined with material. Out of respect to the few original architectural features remaining, the arrangement took on the appearance of a provisional exhibition space. Today the room is largely kept free to provide space for temporary shows, although some important works are on permanent display along the walls. At the end of the nineteenth century the remains of glass frames from the second half of the fourteenth century were placed on the windows of the central chapel; these frames once decorated the minor apses of the church of Santi Giovanni e Paolo.

1-4

Venetian School of the End of the Fifteenth Century
1. *Kneeling Angel with a Candlestick*
2. *Kneeling Angel with a Censer*
3. *Kneeling Angel with a Boat*
4. *Kneeling Angel with a Candlestick*
Saccharoidal marble, height: 100 cm, 104 cm, 106 cm, 98 cm
Cats. S 8, S 9, S 10, S 11
Acquisition: 1922
Latest restoration: 1980

These pieces reflect the influence of Pietro Lombardo, and were likely part of an altar or a grave monument. In August of 1849 the Fabbriceria di San Marco delivered them to the Archaeological Museum, from whence the Accademia received them.

Room 23

5

The Carità Triptychs
On the side walls of the apse are four triptychs that were originally in the church of the Carità, on the altars of the noble chapels up against the "barco." These altars were erected between 1460 and 1464, and consecrated in 1471. Traditionally attributed to Vivarini, these triptychs were later linked to the Bellini ambit, in particular Jacopo's studio. Records exist of drawings made in

collaboration with Giovanni or rather, with Gentile and Giovanni dating the work to the late 1470s. The archaic use of a gold ground could be attributed to the work of assistants from Murano or to the wishes of the commissioners. Nevertheless, the overall form of the works, with the lunettes above, borrowed from Mantegna's altarpiece for San Zeno in Verona, must have had a great impact on Venetian artistic culture.

Jacopo Bellini, Gentile Bellini, Giovanni Bellini and Collaborators
(recorded in Venice from 1424–1470/71; Venice 1429-1507; Venice 1434/39–1516)
5. *Saint Lawrence and Saints John the Baptist and Anthony of Padua Triptych*; in the lunette *Madonna and Child with Angels* Panel, gold ground, 103 × 45 cm (Saints Lawrence and John the Baptist), 127 × 48 cm

(Saint Anthony), 57 × 188 cm (the lunette, divided at the back into three parts) Cat. 621/B
Acquisition: 1812 (Saints Lawrence and the Baptist), following the suppressions; 1834 (Saint Anthony) from the depository of San Giovanni Evangelista; 1923 (the Madonna) and 1954 (the two angels), from the depository of San Giovanni Evangelista from where, in 1840,

6

they were deposited
with the Museo Correr
Latest restoration: 2000

Originally on the altar
of the chapel of Lorenzo
Dolfin, dedicated to Saint
Anthony of Padua and to
Saint Stephen. The general
arrangement appears
influenced by Donatello,
especially with the typology
of the three saints. Giovanni's
intervention is most evident
in the Madonna and Saint
Lawrence.

**Jacopo Bellini,
Gentile Bellini,
Giovanni Bellini
and Collaborators**
(recorded in Venice
from 1424–1470/71;
Venice 1429-1507;
Venice 1434/39–1516)
6. *Nativity and Saints
Francis and Victor Triptych*;
in the lunette *Trinity
between Saints Ubaldo
and Dominic*
Panel, gold ground,
103 × 45 cm (Nativity),
127 × 48 cm (Saints

Francis and Victor),
60 × 166 cm (lunette)
Cat. 621
Acquisition: 1834 (the saints)
from the depositary
of San Giovanni Evangelista;
1891 (Nativity) from Brera
Collection; 1923 (the
lunette), from the Correr
Museum where it had
been deposited, since 1840
Latest restoration: 2000

This piece formed the
altarpiece of the Natività
chapel, belonging to Andrea

Molin. The Trinity in the
lunette is based on a drawing
by Jacopo (British Museum,
folio 56), while the manger
scene appears to have
been modeled after
Vivarini models, such
as the polyptych in Prague,
or that of Conversano
(Room 23, cat. 581, in this
room). The Virgin reveals
the influence of Giovanni
Bellini. On the back
of Saint Victor are sketched
some caricature profiles,
probably by Giovanni.

7

Jacopo Bellini, Gentile Bellini, Giovanni Bellini and Collaborators
(recorded in Venice from 1424–1470/71; Venice 1429–1507; Venice 1434/39–1516)
7. *Virgin and Child with Saint Jerome and Saint Louis of Toulouse* (or *Ubaldo*) Triptych;
in the lunette *Christ in Pietà with Two Angels*
Panels, with gold ground, 127 × 48 cm (each),

60 × 166 cm (lunette)
Cat. 621/C
Acquisition: 1834 (Madonna and Saints) from the depository of San Giovanni Evangelista; 1927 (lunette) from the Brera Gallery
Latest restoration: 2000

Originally in the chapel of Sant'Orsola which, after being sold to Andrea Molin and from him to Zuane Palestrina, belonged to Giacomo Zorzi. The missing

depiction of the title saint has continued to cause perplexity among critics, but was probably due to the fact that at the first meeting with Molin, the ancona provided for five compartments, which were then reduced to only three.

8

Jacopo Bellini, Gentile Bellini, Giovanni Bellini and Collaborators
(recorded in Venice from 1424–1470/71; Venice 1429–1507; Venice 1434/39–1516)
8. *Saint Sebastian with Saint John the Baptist and Saint Anthony Abbot Triptych*; in the lunette *Eternal Father and the Annunciation*
Panel, gold ground, 103 × 45 cm (Saint Sebastian and Saint Anthony),

127 × 48 cm (John the Baptist), 59 × 170 cm (lunette)
Cat. 621/A
Acquisition: 1821 (Saint Sebastian and Saint Anthony); 1834 (John the Baptist) from the depository of San Giovanni Evangelista; 1919 (lunette) with the Austrian restitutions
Latest restoration: 2000

Once the altarpiece in the chapel of San Sebastiano

by Zaccaria Vitturi. It is an exact recomposition of the three panels below and they are linked together by the landscapes. It is held to be the most significant triptych. The figure of Saint Anthony Abbot is a strong reminder of the drawing by Giovanni Bellini in the Royal Library at Windsor, and seems to have been inspired by *San Prosdocimo* by Donatello in the Basilica of Sant'Antonio in Padua.

Notwithstanding the persisting gold ground, the spatial articulation of the images and the chromatic beauty demonstrate an awareness of the latest in Venetian and Paduan art.

9

Gentile Bellini
(Venice 1429-1507)
9. *The Blessed Lorenzo Giustiniani*
Canvas, 221 × 155 cm
Cat. 570
Acquisition: 1852, from the church of Madonna dell'Orto
Latest restoration: 2004–05

On the inscription at the lower center is the date 1465 and the signature. From the church of Madonna dell'Orto, this painting was definitively displayed only in 1887. It may have been a processional standard and was perhaps water-damaged at an unknown date, which would explain the poor condition of the work. This is the first dated piece by Gentile, painted nine years after the death of the first patriarch of Venice. Analysis of the profile of the ascetic, while further denouncing the influence of Andrea Mantegna, also reveals the artist's knack for objective painting, an ability which will eventually lead to his appointment as the official painter of the Republic.

Bartolomeo Giolfino
(Verona ca. 1410–ca. 1486)
10. *Madonna and Child Enthroned with Saints Nicholas (?), John the Baptist, John the Evangelist and Francis*;
(lower order)
Incoronation of the Virgin and Saints George (?), Peter, Jerome and Lorenzo;
(upper order)
Sculpted and painted wood, 380 × 187 cm
Cat. S 2
Acquisition: 1909, by purchase
Latest restoration: 2000

On the scroll on the base is the fragmented inscription with the signature and the date of 1470. From the oratory of the Querini Palazzo in Pressana (near Verona), with the Querini coat of arms on the base itself. The work has lost much of its original color, but the engraving work—also fragmentary—is a highly refined example of Gothic style.

10

11

Bartolomeo Vivarini
(Murano ca. 1430–recorded until 1491)
11. *Madonna Enthroned Adoring the Sleeping Child with Saints Andrea, John the Baptist, Dominic and Peter*
Panels, gold ground,
131 × 49 cm (central),
107 × 33 cm (sides)
Cat. 615
Acquisition: 1812, following the suppressions
Latest restoration: 1994

In the center compartment toward the bottom is the signature and date of 1464. The polyptych comes from the church of Sant'Andrea on the island of Certosa, where it was placed at the altar of the Ca' Morosini chapel. An engraving by G. Sasso provides testimony of the now lost frame with a Crucifixion engraved among the half-figures of prophets. This is one of the most important works by the artist; the Virgin and Child will be alluded to by Giovanni Bellini in his *Madonna Enthroned Adoring the Sleeping Child* (Room 13, cat. 591).

12

Maestro della Madonna del Parto
(recorded between 1390 and ca. 1410)
12. *Madonna del Parto with Two Devotees*
Panel, 188 × 138 cm
Cat. 1328
Acquisition: 1916, on deposit from the church of Santa Caterina
Latest restoration: 1996

On the open book is an invocation to the Virgin Mary, Madonna del Parto. The work is from the late fourteenth century and comes from the church of Santa Caterina. Similar to early works by Nicolò di Pietro, this panel was probably painted in Venice, although it was previously attributed to an Emilian artist.

13   14   16   17

Alvise Vivarini
(Murano 1442/43–died
between 1504 and November
of 1505)
13. *Beatified Martyr*
14. *Saint Claire*
Panels,
143 × 40 cm, 144 × 38 cm
Cats. 593/A, 593)

Acquisition: 1919 (*Beatified
Martyr*) with the Austrian
restitutions ; 1828
(*Saint Claire*), following
the suppressions
Latest restoration: 1948
(*Saint Claire*)

Recorded by Boschini (1664)

in the church of San Daniele,
originally used by
Benedictine nuns, and from
1437 by Augustinian nuns.
Chiara Ogniben Sustan was
responsible for the change
of order; the psychologically
charged face of Saint Claire
(Chiara) has led some critics

to suggest that this may be
a portrait of Chiara Ogniben
Sustan. The position of the
green curtains on the two
panels implies that they
were two independent works
and not part of a larger
piece. The works date
from 1485–90.

Alvise Vivarini
(Murano 1442/43–died
between 1504 and November
of 1505)
15. *Madonna and Child
Enthroned with Saints Louis
of Toulouse, Anthony
of Padua, Anne, Joachim,
Francis and Bernard of Siena*
Panel, 175 × 196 cm
Cat. 607
Acquisition: 1812,
following the suppressions
Latest restoration: 1993

On the base of the throne
is the date 1480 and the
signature. The work was
originally on the altar
of Santa Maria della Prà,
and then on the altar of San
Bernardino in the church
of San Francesco in Treviso,
which the minor friars made
beautiful with works by
Venetian artists—including
Giovanni Mansueti and
Carpaccio—over the fifteenth
and sixteenth centuries
(Quadreria cats. 97 and 90).
The painting is a
masterpiece: the green

15

curtain behind, while still quite old, was added at a later date and is of a material that X-ray analyses have not been able to penetrate. The composition must have originally been arranged with the windows opening on to the landscape, as in the *Madonna Adoring the Sleeping Child* in the church of San Giovanni in Bragora. The bust of Saint Anthony also appears on a panel in the Museo Correr.

Bartolomeo Vivarini
(Murano ca. 1430–recorded until 1491)
16. *Saint Mary Magdalene*
17. *Saint Barbara*
Panels, 132 × 48 cm each
Cats. 584, 585
Acquisition: 1812, following the suppressions
Latest restoration: 1979

The signature and date (1490) appear on the scroll on the lower part of Saint Barbara. These two works come from the now destroyed church of San Geminiano in Venice. They are from the later period of the artist's life, and present a monumentality that foreshadows the next century.

Bartolomeo Vivarini
(Murano ca. 1430–recorded until 1491)
18. *Saint Ambrose Blessing the Brothers, with Saints Louis IX, Peter, Paul and Sebastian*
Panel, gold ground,

19

125 × 47 cm (central), 108 × 36 cm (sides)
Cat. 825
Acquisition: 1919, with the Austrian restitutions
Latest restoration: 1997

On the lower part of Saint Peter are the signature and date (1477); on the lower part of Saint Paul is the signature of the creator of the lost frame: Giacomo da Faenza. This polyptych comes from the Tagliapietra (Stonecutters) Confraternity, and was probably a devotional piece by donation from some members and dedicated to

their personal saints, as the inscription under Saint Ambrose would indicate. The work has a surprisingly impressionistic effect, with an equally strong use of color.

Lazzaro Bastiani
(Venice ca. 1425/30–1512)
19. *Nativity Scene with Saints Eustacius, James, Mark, and Nicholas*
Panel, 160 × 191 cm
Cat. 100
Acquisition: 1812, following the suppressions
Latest restoration: 1994

Originally in the church

of Sant'Elena. The painting was completed according to the will of Eustachio Balbi, who died in 1480. The design of the dwelling seems inspired by similar settings painted by Jacopo Bellini in the books of drawings in the Louvre and the British Museum. The unusual format of the piece is similar to the *Madonna and Child Enthroned* by Alvise Vivarini (Room 23, cat. 607), dating from 1480. The artist's illusionistic ability to create extreme depth through the structure of the dwelling is impressive.

18

20

Andrea da Murano
(recorded from 1463 to 1504)
20. *Saints Vincent Ferreri
and Roch with Saints
Sebastian and Peter the
Martyr*; in the lunette,
*Madonna della Misericordia
with Saints Louis IX (?),
Dominic, Thomas Aquinas
and Catherine of Siena*
Canvas transferred from a
panel, 152 × 88 cm (central
panel), panel, 152 × 47 cm

(sides), panel, 80 × 199 cm
(lunette)
Acquisition: 1812,
following the suppressions;
1883, Brera Gallery
(central panel)
Cat. 28
Latest restoration: 1948

Signed at the lower center,
this triptych was originally
in the church of San Pietro
Martire on Murano.

All of the saints represented
on the lower order—including
Saint Peter, after whom
the church was named—are
venerated for their magical
qualities against the plague;
Saint Roch indicates a bubo
under his clothing, while
the small devotees and
commissioners kneeling
seem to be praying for
protection against contagion.
The artist was an attentive

observer of the artistic trends
developing in those years
in the area of the Venetian
lagoon, and was among
the few Venetians who
truly understood the work
of Andrea del Castagno.
The work was surely painted
in relation to a plague,
probably the one of 1478.

Carlo Crivelli
(Venice 1430/35–died
between August 7, 1494,
and September, 1495
21. *Saints Peter and Paul*
22. *Saints Ansovinus (?)
and Jerome*
Panels, 218 × 54 cm,
187 × 72 cm

Cats. 103, 103/A
Acquisition: 1883, from
the Brera Gallery (*Saints
Ansovinus [?] and Jerome*);
1895 (*Saints Peter and Paul*)
by purchase
Latest restoration: 1979

Originally part of a large
polyptych, the two panels
were located in the Cathedral
of Camerino, where they
were placed alongside the
Madonna della Candeletta
(Milan, Brera Gallery).
The church was destroyed
by an earthquake in 1799,
and the *Madonna* and *Saints
Ansovinus (?) and Jerome*
were taken to the Brera
Gallery in Milan; the latter
panel came to the Accademia
through an exchange (1883).
The bishop can be identified
as Ansovinus, patron saint
of the city of Camerino.
The panel with *Saints Peter
and Paul* seems to have
been recovered from under
the rubble of the church,
passed into the collection
of Servanzi Collio and
then sold to the State (1895).
In spite of the fact that
the expressionism of the
saints seems to be in contrast
with the formal elegance
of the Madonna, the pieces
were part of a single
complex, as is shown by
the similar dimensions and
the repetition of the identical
parapet. As the central
panel is signed with the title
of *eques*, an honor bestowed
upon the painter in 1490
by prince Ferdinando
of Capua, the paintings
should correspond to around
that date.

**Bartolomeo Vivarini
and Workshop**
(Murano ca. 1430–recorded
until 1491)
23. *Conversano Polyptych*
Panels, 154 × 46 cm (central),
138 × 23 cm (sides), 25 × 270
cm (predella), 46 × 45 cm
(cyma)
Cat. 581
Acquisition: 1883, by
purchase from the
Conversano cathedral
Latest restoration: 1995

The central panel depicts
the Nativity between Saints
Francis, Andrew, John the
Baptist, Peter, Paul, Jerome,
Dominic and Theodore.
In the cyma Christ passes
between two angels; the
predella has Christ with the
apostles. At the bottom, in
the Nativity, is an inscription
with the date 1475, while
on the fillet of the frame of
the predella appear another
inscription and the artist's
signature. The work's
destination in far-off Puglia
seems to have led the artist
to treat this as a less
important commission.
While the central group
translates the figures painted
by Antonio Vivarini for a 1447
polyptych (today in Prague)
into stronger and more tactile
forms, the saints at the sides
and the predella seem weaker
and by different hands.

21

22

23

Canvases from the Sala dell'Albergo of the Scuola Grande di San Marco

The five canvases located at the back of the church were part of the original decoration of the Sala dell'Albergo (hall) of the Scuola di San Marco, together with the *Sermon of Saint Mark at Alexandria* by Gentile Bellini and the *Baptism of Saint Mark* by Giovanni Mansueti, today in the Brera Gallery. In 1492 Gentile and Giovanni Bellini offered to paint the room, and came to an agreement with the Scuola. However, Gentile died in 1507 without finishing the *Sermon*, which was completed by Giovanni. In 1515 the Scuola hired Giovanni to paint the *Martyrdom of Saint Mark*, but unfortunately on November 29, 1516, the artist died and the work was left unfinished until Vittore Belliniano completed it in 1526. Later works were commissioned from Giovanni Mansueti, collaborator and disciple of Gentile Bellini, thus guaranteeing the stylistic continuity of the cycle. Mansueti died in 1526 or 1527, and the last two paintings, the *Presentation of Saint Mark's Ring* by Paris Bordon, and the *Saints Mark, George and Nicholas Freeing Venice from Demons (Sea Storm)* by Palma il Vecchio, reveal a radical change in the taste of the commissioners. When the Scuola was suppressed by Napoleonic decree in 1806, the cycle was dispersed, with pieces in Milan, Venice and Vienna. The works in Vienna were returned in 1919 and the cycle was reassembled at the Accademia Galleries in 1994 (but without the paintings in the Brera).

25

24

232

**Giovanni Bellini
and Vittore Belliniano**
(Venice 1434/39–1516);
recorded in Venice from 1507
to 1529)
24. *Martyrdom of Saint
Mark*
Canvas, 362 × 771 cm
(the central cut at door level
is 158 × 272 cm)
Cat. 1002
Acquisition: 1919, with
the Austrian restitutions
Latest restoration: 1987–94

On July 4, 1515, the Scuola
commissioned Giovanni
Bellini to paint a canvas
with the story of Saint Mark,
who "… in Alexandria was
dragged along the ground by
those infidel Moors." This is
the scene of the martyrdom
that appears in the Marciani
mosaics: during the Easter
feast Mark's adversaries
had sent soldiers to arrest the
saint; dragging him by a cord
tied around his neck they
went through the streets of
Alexandria for the entire day
and until the next morning

when he died. The paintings
in the Doge's Palace have
been lost, so this is one
of the very rare examples
of the artist's larger decorative
works, although it was not
painted entirely by him.
In fact, when Giovanni
died on November 19, 1516,
the work was completed
by Vittore Belliniano,
Bellini's co-worker in the
Doge's Palace, who placed
his signature on it and the
date of 1526, ten years later.
The drawing and preparation
of the great canvas are
doubtless the work of
Giovanni based on a sketch
by his brother, but the actual
painting on the canvas was
by Vittore. Perhaps, as recent
critics have proposed, he also
had the collaboration of
Lorenzo Lotto, who was a
guest of the convent of Santi
Giovanni e Paolo, attached
to the Scuola di San Marco,
from 1525 to 1526. But
it is clear that Bellini was
responsible for the view
with Saint Cyriac of Ancona

in the background on
the hill, which is similar
to the one that appears
on Niccolini's *Crucifixion*
which is now in Prato.

Giovanni Mansueti
(recorded in Venice
from 1485–died between
September 1526, and
March 1527)
25. *Saint Mark Heals Aniano*
Canvas, 370 × 407 cm
Cat. 569
Acquisition: 1838,
with the suppressions
Latest restoration: 1992–94

This painting and the
Baptism of Aniano, today in
the Brera Gallery, surely refer
to the "doi telleri in albergo"
(the two canvases in the Sala
dell'Albergo) that the Scuola
decided to have painted
on October 24, 1518.
Gentile Bellini died in 1507,
Giovanni in 1516, and Vittore
Belliniano was still occupied
on his *Martyrdom* so
Mansueti, a disciple primarily
of Gentile, whose drawings

he had worked on, with his
somewhat behind-the-times
taste must have seemed a
logical choice to guarantee
the stylistic unity of the cycle.
The Guardian Grande
Antonio de Maistri
commissioned the piece,
assigning the third canvas
to Mansueti in 1525,
presumably the year when
the two paintings were
completed. This painting
was located "on the left
upon entering," after the
*Saints Mark, George and
Nicholas Freeing Venice from
Demons* (*Sea Storm*) and the
*Presentation of Saint Mark's
Ring* (Room 23, respectively
cats. 516 and 320). It depicts
an episode in the life
of Saint Mark. When he
reached Alexandria, he
breaks a strap on his sandal
and the archangel Michael
appears to him and has Mark
follow him so he can show
Mark his successor. Mark
finds the cobbler Aniano
and gives the sandal to him.
While Aniano is repairing
the sandal, he injures his left
hand, which Mark heals with
his saliva mixed with dust
from the street. The scene
takes place within an
interesting architectural
context; the building at the
back with the veiled women
recalls the *Prayer*, now
in the Brera Gallery, and
the descriptions of Vasari
of a lost painting by Alvise
Vivarini in the Sala del
Maggior Consiglio; the
decorations of this Sala
were the inspiration for the
entire cycle in the Albergo.
An inscription at the center
describes the miracle, while
to the lower left a camel
driver holds a scroll with
the artist's signature.

26

Giovanni Mansueti
(recorded in Venice
from 1485–died between
September 1526 and
March 1527)
26. *Episodes from the Life
of Saint Mark*
(*Plotting of the Idolaters,
Capture during Mass,
Apparition of the Angel
and Christ in Prison*)
Canvas, 371 × 603 cm

Cat. 571
Acquisition: 1838,
following the suppressions
Latest restoration: 1992–94

To the lower left, a child
holds a scroll with the
artist's signature. This work
was originally in the Sala
dell'Albergo between
the two windows, and
was commissioned by the

Guardian Grande Antonio
di Maistri in 1525. When
Mansueti died, between
September 1526 and March
1527, the painting was nearly
finished, although "some
heads" had not yet been
added. The composition is
articulated in three episodes.
To the right, under a loggia,
the idolatrous Egyptians plot
against Mark, envious of his

ever-growing number
of followers. At the center,
the saint is beset by enemies
while celebrating mass and
they then drag him through
the streets of Alexandria.
To the left, he is brought into
jail, where an angel appears
to him to announce his
entrance into a new life.
At this announcement Mark
thanks Christ and prays

for him to receive his soul,
at which point Jesus appears
to him and speaks the
famous words "Pax tibi,
Marce, evangelista meus"
(Peace be with you, Mark,
my Evangelist). According
to the affirmations of his
daughter Cecilia, Mansueti
included the portraits of the
more important members
of the Scuola in the painting.

27

Jacopo Negretti known as Palma il Vecchio and Paris Bordon
(Serina, Bergamo, ca. 1480–Venice 1528; Treviso 1500–Venice 1571)
27. *Saints Mark, George and Nicholas Freeing Venice from Demons*
(*Sea Storm*)
Canvas, 362 × 408 cm
Cat. 516
Acquisition: 1829, following the suppressions
Latest restoration: 1993–94

This work was originally in the Sala dell'Albergo, immediately to the left after entering. The work was almost certainly referred to by the Scuola on November 5, 1534, when the room was described as decorated "with paintings," including "the painting that will be delivered in a few days." It must have remained unfinished or in some way damaged after its completion, as the large insert to the right with the boat containing the fisherman and the three saints would attest; this part has been attributed to Paris Bordon. Before displaying it at the Accademia Galleries in 1830, the part to the lower left with the Saint Peter's fish was also added by Sebastiano Santi in order to fill in the missing part corresponding to a doorway. This painting and the following one depict the legend of a terrible storm with very high seas that occurred on the night of February 25, 1341. An old fisherman found shelter under a bridge in the place that was then called Terranova, where the public granaries were located and where the formerly royal gardens are now. A man came to the fisherman from the nearby church of San Marco, and asked the fisherman to take him to the island of San Giorgio, where another stranger also boarded the boat. They then went towards San Nicolò del Lido, where a third person came aboard. While the storm raged on, Saint Mark, Saint George and Saint Nicholas all appeared to the fisherman. Suddenly a large galley containing countless devils appeared in the churning sea before them and headed towards Venice to destroy the city. The three angels intervened and sent the ship to the bottom of the sea. Before returning into his church as the other saints had done, Mark gave the astonished fisherman a ring to give to the Doge as proof of the events he had witnessed.
The sailboat at the center was inspired by a drawing by Lorenzo Lotto for one of the inlaid wood pieces of Santa Maria Maggiore in Bergamo. The authorship of the painting, whose identification was always

28

problematic, has been
made difficult by the many
changes and additions made
to the piece. In 1550 Vasari
attributed it to Giorgione,
but in the 1568 edition
he attributed it to Palma.
It is probable that after
the death of Mansueti
between 1527 and 1528,
the painting was indeed
entrusted to Palma, who
was a member of the Scuola
from 1513 until his death
on July 30, 1528. The work
was probably commissioned
in the years immediately
prior to this date, and
so he may not have had
the time to finish the canvas,
which instead was completed
or repaired by Paris Bordon
in 1534.

Paris Bordon
(Treviso 1500–Venice 1571)
28. *Presentation of Saint
Mark's Ring*
Canvas, transferred
from another canvas,
370 × 300 cm
Cat. 320
Acquisition: 1815,
following the suppressions,
with the restitutions
from Paris
Latest restoration: 1988

This painting was originally
in the Sala dell'Albergo,
on the left of the entrance,
between *Saints Mark, George
and Nicholas Freeing Venice
from Demons* and *Saint
Mark Heals Aniano*.
The work is related to the
Scuola's decision on January

12, 1534 to have made
"uno o doi teleri" ("one or
two paintings"), for which
a competition was held.
On the base of the pillar
at right is the signature.
The work shows the
fisherman who offers the
ring of Saint Mark—which
tradition still holds as
being among the treasures
of the Basilica—to the Doge
as proof of the miraculous
events of the night before.
Surrounding Doge Andrea
Gritti are the senators,
while on the left is the
Great Guardian and
a group of members of the
confraternity. The complex
architectural setting of the
background—suggestive
of the Doge's Palace—was

inspired by Sebastiano Serlio.
The decision of 1534
notwithstanding, this
painting, which was
enthusiastically praised
by Vasari, dates to the early
1540s, as is evidenced by its
adhesion to the teachings
of Titian and of the Tuscan
artists in Venice at that time.

Room 23

24 The Former Sala dell'Albergo
of the Scuola di Santa Maria della Carità

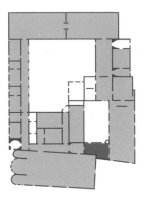

This was the Sala dell'Albergo of the Scuola di Santa Maria della Carità, where the most highly ranked members met, and where the registers, charters (called the "mariegola"), and the relics were all kept. The ceiling, gilt and multicolored, with the four Evangelists, dates from the end of the fifteenth century. The Holy Father at the center was probably taken from a previous ceiling in the Assembly Hall which may have been destroyed by fire. In 1811 Selva opened the short stairway; for this occasion the wooden altar was disassembled and the triptych by Antonio Vivarini and Giovanni d'Alemagna was moved to the right wall.

Titian
*Presentation of Mary
at the Temple*, detail

**Antonio Vivarini and
Giovanni d'Alemagna**
(Murano ca. 1418/20–1476/84;
recorded from 1441 to 1450)
1. *Madonna and Child
Enthroned with Saints
Jerome, Gregory, Ambrose
and Augustine*
Canvas,
344 × 203 cm (central),
344 × 137 cm (sides)
Cat. 625
Acquisition: 1807,
following the suppressions
Latest restoration: 1999

On the step of the throne
is written the signature and
the date 1446. This work
was painted for the Sala
dell'Albergo, for the wall in
front of Titian's *Presentation
of Mary at the Temple*
(Room 24, cat. 626),
where the inserted wooden
frame was destroyed
along with the altar in 1811,
when the connecting
access was opened.
One of the oldest Venetian
paintings on canvas, it is
certainly the most unified
work of those attributed
to the two artists. This makes
it difficult to distinguish
the part each had in its
composition. The Virgin and
angels are clearly attributable
to Vivarini. The new notions
about perspective are evident
in spite of the abundance
of decoration, which must
have appeared even more
opulent when completed
with the original frames.
These notions probably
reflect the artists' awareness
of the graphic studies
Donatello made in
preparation for the saint's
altar in Padua.

1

2

Tiziano Vecellio known as Titian
(Pieve di Cadore ca. 1488/90–Venice 1576)
2. *Presentation of Mary at the Temple*
Canvas, 335 × 775 cm
Cat. 626
Acquisition: 1807, following the suppressions
Latest restoration: 1981

This large canvas was painted for the Sala dell'Albergo of the Scuola della Carità between August 1534 and March 1539. The walls of the room were also decorated to the left by the *Marriage of the Virgin* by Giampietro Silvio, and to the right by Girolamo Dente's *Annunciation*, still in storage at the parish

of Mason Vicentino and now in the storerooms of the Galleries. The painting appears to have been cut below to accommodate the two doors. The door to the observer's right already existed and was probably the Gothic doorway, today walled over, which was the old entrance of the ground floor room. The left door was opened on March 10, 1572, while Titian was still alive, and required the sacrifice of part of the canvas. Although the horizontal path of the wall incorporates a certain design taken from the Venetian narrative tradition—and mostly from Carpaccio—the master does so with a remarkably "modern" spirit

and a deep awareness of the contemporary architectural notions proposed by Sansovino and Serlio. The perfect balance between architecture and landscape, and of both together with the open procession of the members of the confraternity, firmly establishes the unity of the work, a new interpretation of the fifteenth century models and of great importance for the painters who followed.

3   4

**Veneto-Byzantine School
of the Fourteenth and
Fifteenth Centuries**
3. *Reliquary of Cardinal
Bessarione*
Wood, silver, gilt filigree,
enamel, glass and precious
stones, 47 × 32 cm
Cat. S 19
Acquisition: 1919, with the
suppression of the Scuola,
it first entered the collection
of Luigi Savorgnan and later
that of Abbot Luigi Celotti,
who sold it to the Emperor
Francis I in 1821;
1919, assigned to the
Galleries with the Austrian
restitutions

Donated to the Scuola della
Carità in 1463 by Cardinal
Bessarione, the famous
scholar who with the bequest
of his manuscripts brought

about the institution of the
Marciana library. This piece,
which even Gentile Bellini
helped to construct, was
originally located in a
tabernacle (now dispersed)
on the altar on the wall
where now the short stairway
begins. The precious piece is
formed of a cross with Christ
encased on an enameled
tablet which includes four
rock crystal cases containing
the "Holy Wood" and "Holy
Shroud" relics, two plates
with the archangels Gabriel
and Michael, Constantine
and Saint Helena painted
on glass, a cover composed
of a fixed part framing
the reliquary on three sides
with seven small scenes from
the Passion and a moveable
shutter cover on which
the Crucifixion is depicted.

The origin and date
of the rare and complex
work is problematic; not
only because of the difficulty
of interpreting the Greek
and Latin inscriptions, but
also because the embedding
for the cross and the painted
cover are probably the work
of Bessarione.

**Sixteenth-Century
Veneto Painter**
4. *Portrait of Cardinal
Bessarione*
Canvas, 116 × 95 cm
Cat. 876
Acquisition: 1807,
following the suppressions
Latest restoration: 1969

Originally in the Sala
dell'Albergo, this painting
was commissioned by
the Scuola della Carità
on March 8, 1540. Cardinal
Bessarione is depicted
holding the reliquary given
to him by the Scuola itself
and wearing the apparel
of a member of the
confraternity.

5

**Sixteenth Century
Venetian School**
5. *Doge Sebastiano Ziani
Meets Pope Alexander III
at the Church of Santa Maria
della Carità*
Canvas, 185 × 234 cm
Cat. 654
Acquisition: 1884, from
the Doge's Palace
Latest restoration: 1963

This painting may originally
have been in the Carità
church. It depicts Doge Ziani
meeting Pope Alexander III.
According to legend, the
pope had come to Venice
while fleeing Barbarossa.
The piece is also interesting
for documentary reasons,
as it shows how the façade
of the church and the Scuola
appeared around the middle
of the sixteenth century.

The "Quadreria" Gallery

In the early 1970s on the top floor of the Palladian Monastery, the Accademia Galleries were provided with a repository created with two aims in mind: a secondary gallery in the long corridor, and a room for consultation in a spacious enclosed environment, with the paintings arranged on fixed metal trellises. The long, elegant corridor was conceived by Andrea Palladio as an entranceway to the cells of the large religious order, the Lateran Canons for whom he had "tried to make this abode like that of the Ancients." Access to it is afforded from the oval stairway of which the architect himself wrote: "I made of it an empty place in the middle of the Monastero della Carità in Venice that is truly admirable." Indeed, as he had predicted in his treatise, "when standing atop the stairway, one can see—and be seen by—everyone who ascends or begins to ascend." These structural works belonging now to the distant past, both the stairway and corridor were in need of full restoration, and the paintings required a more fitting position. By fortuitous coincidence, the restoration works of 1995 were undertaken at almost the same time as the restoration of the terracotta façade, dated 1561, and of the tablinum, which in the house of the ancients was the space dedicated to the Penates, or household gods, and used as a vestry.

The long corridor has been conceived as a type of storeroom, which is organized chronologically with suitable lighting and fittings. Here, about eighty paintings are found and can be viewed not just by scholars but also by all visitors, upon prior booking.

Tiziano Vecellio known as Titian and Workshop
(Pieve di Cadore ca. 1488/90–Venice 1576)
Symbol of Saint Luke (Bull)
Symbol of Saint Matthew (Angel)
Symbol of Saint Mark (Lion)
Symbol of Saint John (Eagle)
Panels, 45.5 × 236 cm,
49.5 × 203 cm, 45.5 × 240 cm,
49.5 × 198 cm
Cats. 1035a, 1035b, 1035c, 1035d
Acquisition: 1812,
following the suppressions
Latest restoration: 1989

Cherub Head
Panel, 45 × 40 cm
Cat. 1035m
Acquisizione: 1812,
following the suppressions
Laest restoration: 1989

Two Cherub Heads
Panel, 40.5 × 46.5 cm
Cat. 1035t
Acquisition: 1812,
following the suppressions
Latest restoration: 1989

Mask of Satyr
Panel, 59 × 58 cm
Cat. 1035h
Acquisition: 1812,
following the suppressions
Latest restoration: 1989

Face of a Woman
Panel, 49 × 43 cm
Cat. 1035o
Acquisition: 1812,
following the suppressions
Latest restoration: 1989

Paris Bordon
(Treviso 1500–Venice 1571)
Winged Putti with Garlands
Panel, 52 × 101 cm
Cat. 311
Acquisition: 1816, from the
bequest of Girolamo Molin
Latest restoration: 1980

Bonifacio de' Pitati known as Bonifacio Veronese
(Verona 1487–Venice 1553)
Christ and the Apostles
Panel, 189 × 151 cm
Cat. 309
Acquisition: 1814,
following the suppressions
Latest restoration: 1955

The Visiting Angel
Canvas, 198 × 135 cm
Cat. 942
Acquisition: 1919, with
the Austrian restitutions
Latest restoration: 1963

The Virgin
Canvas, 197 × 137 cm
Cat. 943
Acquisition: 1919, with
the Austrian restitutions
Latest restoration: 1963

Andrea Meldolla known as Schiavone
(Zara ca. 1510/15–Venice 1563)
Christ before Pilate
Canvas, 104 × 170 cm
Cat. 271
Acquisition: 1850, from the
bequest of Felicita Renier
Latest restoration: 1956

Jacopo Robusti known as Jacopo Tintoretto
(Venice 1519–1594)
*The Crucifixions
on Mount Ararat*
Incomplete panel, 138 × 218 cm
Cat. 1091
Acquisition: 1865,
following the suppressions
Latest restoration: 1960

Saint Peter
Canvas, 104 × 33 cm
Cat. 506
Acquisition: 1838, by donation
from Girolamo Contarini
Latest restoration: 1960

Saint Paul
Canvas, 104 × 33 cm
Cat. 501
Acquisition: 1838, by donation
from Girolamo Contarini
Latest restoration: 1960

*Presentation of Christ
at the Temple*
Canvas, 237 × 296 cm
Cat. 725
Acquisition: 1960, by decree
Latest restoration: 1986

The Deposition
Canvas, 227 × 294 cm
Cat. 217
Acquisition: 1806,
following the suppressions
Latest restoration: 1989

Jacopo da Ponte known as Jacopo Bassano
(Bassano ca. 1510/15–1592)
Saint Jerome
Canvas, 119 × 154 cm
Cat. 652
Acquisition: 1900, by purchase

Jacopo da Ponte known as Jacopo Bassano, Workshop
(Bassano ca. 1510/15–1592)
Adoration of the Shepherds
Canvas, 120 × 222 cm
Cat. 902
Acquisition: 1933, from the State
depository of the Doge's Palace
Latest restoration: 1956

Jacopo da Ponte known as Jacopo Bassano, and Assistants

(Bassano ca. 1510/15–1592)

Virgin and Child Enthroned in Glory with Saint Jerome
Canvas, 220 × 161 cm
Cat. 920
Acquisition: 1930, from the State depository
Latest restoration: 1963

Paolo Caliari known as Paolo Veronese

(Verona 1528–1588)
Assumption of the Virgin

Canvas, 396 x 200 cm
Cat. 265
Acquisition: 1812, following the suppressions
Latest restoration: 1988

Paolo Caliari known as Paolo Veronese, Workshop

(Verona 1528–1588)

Madonna of the Rosary
Canvas, 173 × 316 cm
Cat. 207
Acquisition: 1844, following the suppressions
Latest restoration: 1986–87

Carlo Caliari

(Venice 1570–1596)

Saint Augustine Dictating His "Rules" to the Lateran Canons
Canvas, 285 × 146 cm
Cat. 813
Acquisition: 1919, with the Austrian restitutions

Domenico Robusti known as Domenico Tintoretto

(Venice 1560–1635)

Two Portraits of Confreres from the Scuola dei Mercanti
Canvases, 330 × 194 cm each
Cats. 872, 873
Acquisition: 1919, with the Austrian restitutions
Latest restoration: 1956

Veneto Painter of the Early-Seventeenth Century

Two Young Women Playing the Guitar
An Old Man and a Young Woman

Detached frescoes, 107 × 122 cm, 106 × 122 cm
Cats. 731, 733
Acquisition: 1827, following its removal prior to the demolition of the building which housed it
Latest restoration: 1995

Jacopo Negretti known as Palma il Giovane

(Venice 1548–1628)

Susanna and the Elders
Canvas, 96 × 79 cm
Cat. 538
Acquisition: 1838, by donation from Girolamo Contarini
Latest restoration: 1955

The Pleasures of the Prodigal Son
Canvas, 83 × 118 cm
Cat. 634
Acquisition: 1838, by donation from Girolamo Contarini
Latest restoration: 1958

Return of the Prodigal Son
Canvas, 83 × 118 cm
Cat. 684
Acquisition: 1838, by donation from Girolamo Contarini
Latest restoration: 1958

Dead Christ Held by Three Angels
Canvas, 130 × 108 cm
Cat. 267
Acquisition: 1850, from the bequest of Felicita Renier
Latest restoration: 1994

Alessandro Varotari known as Padovanino

(Padua 1590–Venice 1650)

Frieze with Putti
Canvas, 495 × 97 cm
Cat. 802
Acquisition: 1835, from the State depository
Latest restoration: 1962

Orpheus and Eurydice
Canvas, 164 × 119 cm
Cat. 548
Acquisition: 1838, by donation from Girolamo Contarini
Latest restoration: 1994

Francesco Maffei

(Vicenza ca. 1605–Padua 1660)

The Virgin Appears to Saint Filippo Neri
Canvas, 215 × 145 cm
Cat. 1093
Acquisition: 1865, from the State depository
Latest restoration: 1961

Charles Le Brun

(Paris 1619–1690)

Pharisee's Banquet with Christ and Mary Magdalene
Canvas, 386 × 318 cm
Cat. 377
Acquisition: 1815, from France in exchange for *The Wedding at Cana* by Paolo Veronese
Latest restoration: 1962

Nicola Renieri (Nicolas Régnier)

(Maubeuge 1591–Venice 1667)

Allegorical Figure
Canvas, 140 × 68 cm
Cat. 553
Acquisition: 1838, following the suppressions
Latest restoration: 1958

Joseph Heintz the Younger

(Ausburg ca. 1600–Venice 1678)
Four Crowned Saints Refuse to Worship Idols

Canvas, 266 × 169 cm
Cat. 1365
Acquisition: 1982, by purchase

Flemish School of the Early Seventeenth Century

Flowers in a Basket
Flowers in a Bowl
Panels, cm 49 × 69, 47 × 63 cm
Cats. 193, 199
Acquisition: 1816, by donation from Girolamo Molin

Early Seventeenth-Century Painter from Northern Italy (?)

Still Life with Sculpture
Canvas, 80 × 65 cm
Cat. 363
Acquisition: 1838, by donation from Girolamo Contarini
Latest restoration: 1970

Pietro Berrettini known as Pietro da Cortona
(Cortona 1596–Rome 1669)

Daniel in the Lions' Den
Canvas, 440 × 223 cm
Cat. 754
Acquisition: 1829, following the suppressions
Latest restoration: 1955

Luca Giordano
(Naples 1634–1705)

Deposition
Canvas, 440 × 243 cm
Cat. 643
Acquisition: 1829, following the suppressions
Latest restoration: 1961–62

Giulio Carpioni
(Venice? 1613–Vicenza 1679)

Triumph of Silenus
Canvas, 96 × 79 cm
Cat. 739
Acquisition: 1910, by donation from Giuseppe Rossi
Latest restoration: 1956

Sebastiano Mazzoni
(Florence? 1611–Venice 1678)

Mystical Marriage of Saint Catherine
Canvas, 154 × 449 cm
Cat. 1331
Acquisition: 1965, from the church of Santa Caterina
Latest restoration: 2002–03

Saint Catherine Disputing with the Philosophers
Canvas, 167 × 445 cm
Cat. 1330
Acquisition: 1965, from the church of Santa Caterina
Latest restoration: 2002–03

Giovanni Antonio Fumiani
(Venice 1650–1710)

Christ with the Doctors
Canvas, 553 × 314 cm
Cat. 1390
Acquisition: 1988, from the State depository
Latest restoration: 1988–90

Gregorio Lazzarini
(Venice 1655–Villabona 1730)

Circumcision
Canvas, 553 × 314 cm
Cat. 1391
Acquisition: 1988, from the State depository
Latest restoration: 1988–90

Alessandro Magnasco and Anton Francesco Peruzzini
(Genoa ca. 1667–ca. 1749; Ancona 1650/55–Milan 1720/25)

Landscape with Praying Monks (The Great Wood)
Canvas, 174 × 237 cm
Cat. 1389
Acquisition: 1989, by right of purchase

Giambattista Piazzetta
(Venice 1683–1754)

Christ Crucifixed with the Two Thieves
Canvas, 76 × 62 cm
Cat. 719
Acquisition: 1905, by purchase
Latest restoration: 1995

Michele Marieschi
(Venice 1710–1743)

View with Bridge
Canvas, 62 × 95 cm
Cat. 715
Acquisition: 1908, by purchase

Francesco Zugno
(Venice 1709–1787)

Saint Benedict
Canvas, 57.5 × 45.5 cm
Cat. 1347
Acquisition: 1977, by purchase
Latest restoration: 1974–75

Saint Bruno
Canvas, 57.5 × 45.5 cm
Cat. 1348
Acquisition: 1977, by purchase
Latest restoration: 1974–75

Giuseppe Bazzani
(Mantua 1690–1769)
Adoration of the Magi

Canvas, 106 × 79 cm
Cat. 747
Acquisition: 1909, by donation from A. Salvadori
Latest restoration: 1938

Rest in Egypt
Canvas, 106 × 79 cm
Cat. 748
Acquisition: 1909, by donation from A. Salvadori
Latest restoration: 1938

Francesco Hayez
(Venice 1791–Milan 1882)

Destruction of the Temple of Jerusalem
Canvas, 183 × 82 cm
Cat. 756
Acquisition: 1868, by donation from the artist
Latest restoration: 1989

Giambattista Mariotti, attr.
(Venice 1694–Padua ca. 1765)

Saint Ignatius of Loyola Before the Pope
Canvas, 119 × 160 cm
Cat. 1321
Acquisition: 1960, by purchase
Latest restoration: 1960–61

Giandomenico Tiepolo

(Venice 1727–1804)

The Institution of the Eucharist
Canvas, 137 × 100 cm
Cat. 488
Acquisition: 1807, from
the old Accademia
Latest restoration: 1960

Alessandro Longhi

(Venice 1733–1813)

*The Architect Tommaso
Temanza*
Canvas, 72 × 55 cm
Cat. 478
Acquisition: 1845, by donation
from Francesco Lazzari
Latest restoration: 1994

*Portrait of Doge Alvise IV
Mocenigo*
Canvas, 82 × 65 cm
Cat. 473
Acquisition: 1807, from
the old Accademia
Latest restoration: 1958

Portrait of Doge Paolo Renier
Canvas, 81 × 66 cm
Cat. 477
Acquisition: 1807, from
the old Accademia
Latest restoration: 1961

Madonna
Canvas, 44 × 36 cm
Cat. 1332
Acquisition: 1959,
following the suppressions
Latest restoration: 1961

Luigi Crespi

(Bologna 1708–1779)

Self Portrait
Canvas, 114 × 95 cm
Cat. 482
Acquisition: 1807, from
the old Accademia

Domenico Pellegrini

(Galliera Veneta 1759–
Rome 1840)

*Portrait of the Engraver
Francesco Bartolozzi*
Canvas, 106 × 89 cm
Cat. 453
Acquisition: 1834, by donation
from the artist
Latest restoration: 1958

Giovanni Migliara

(Alessandria 1785–Milan 1837)

View of a Shoreside Church
Canvas, 47 × 56 cm
Cat. 710
Acquisition: 1903, by purchase
Latest restoration: 1903

Ippolito Caffi

(Belluno 1809–Lissa 1866)

Fog in Piazza San Marco
Canvas, 36 × 29 cm
Cat. 1155
Acquisition: 1873, by donation
from Giovanni Alvise Pigazzi

Noè Bordignon

(Salvarosa 1841–San Zenone
degli Ezzelini 1920)

*Blind-Man's Bluff in the Roman
Countryside*
Canvas, 73 × 96 cm
Cat. 1169
Acquisition: 1879, by donation
from the artist

Pietro Longhi, exhibition catalogue (Museo Correr, Venice, December 4, 1993–April 4, 1994), edited by A. Mariuz, G. Pavanello, G. Romanelli, Milan 1993.

U. Ruggeri, *Il Padovanino*, Soncino 1993.

Le siècle de Titien. L'âge d'or de la peinture à Venise, exhibition catalogue (Grand Palais, Paris, March 9–June 14, 1993), Paris 1993.

D. Succi, *Francesco Guardi. Itinerario dell'avventura artistica*, Milan 1993.

1994

Bessarione e l'Umanesimo, exhibition catalogue (Biblioteca Nazionale Marciana, Venice, April 27–May 31, 1994), edited by G. Fiaccadori, Naples 1994.

"Giovanni Battista Cima," proceedings from the international study conference (Palazzo Sarcinelli, Conegliano, October 1–2, 1994), edited by P. Humfrey, A. Gentili, in *Venezia Cinquecento*, 7, 1994.

Jacopo Tintoretto. Ritratti, exhibition catalogue (Gallerie dell'Accademia, Venice, March 25–July 10, 1994; Kunsthistorisches Museum, Vienna, July 31–October 30, 1994), Milan 1994.

G. Nepi Scirè, *I teleri della Sala dell'Albergo nella Scuola di San Marco*, Venice 1994.

A. Scarpa Sonino, *Jacopo Amigoni*, Soncino 1994.

1995

A. Ballarin, *Jacopo Bassano. Scritti 1964–1995*, edited by V. Romani, 2 vols., Cittadella 1995.

G. Knox, *Antonio Pellegrini: 1675–1741*, Oxford 1995.

Bernardo Strozzi. Genova 1581/82–Venezia 1644, exhibition catalogue (Palazzo Ducale, Genoa, May 6–August 6, 1995), edited by E. Gavazza, G. Nepi Scirè, G. Rotondi Terminiello, Milan 1995.

L. Mortari, *Bernardo Strozzi*, Rome 1995.

R. Pallucchini, *La pittura nel Veneto. Il Settecento*, edited by M. Lucco, A. Mariuz, G. Pavanello, F. Zava, 2 vols., Milan 1995.

Splendori del Settecento veneziano, exhibition catalogue (Museo del Settecento Veneziano, Ca' Rezzonico, Gallerie dell'Accademia, Palazzo Mocenigo, Venice, May 26–July 30, 1995), edited by G. Nepi Scirè, G. Romanelli, Milan 1995.

T. Pignatti, F. Pedrocco, *Veronese. Catalogo completo*, 2 vols., Milan 1995.

1996

C.E. Cohen, *The art of Giovanni Antonio da Pordenone: between dialect and language*, 2 vols., Cambridge 1996.

Domenico Fetti 1588/89–1623, exhibition catalogue (Palazzo Te, Mantua, September 15–December 15, 1996), edited by E.A. Safarik, Milan 1996.

A. Gentili, *Le Storie di Carpaccio. Venezia, i turchi, gli ebrei*, Venice 1996 (reprint 2006).

Giambattista Tiepolo 1696–1996, exhibition catalogue (Museo del Settecento Veneziano, Venice, Ca' Rezzonico, September 6–December 8, 1996; The Metropolitan Museum of Art, New York, January 24–April 27, 1997), Milan 1996.

Jacopo Tintoretto nel quarto centenario della morte, proceedings of the conference (Venice, November 24–26, 1994), edited by P. Rossi, L. Puppi, Padua 1996.

Alessandro Magnasco: 1667–1749, exhibition catalogue (Palazzo Reale, Milan, March 21–July 7, 1996), edited by M. Bona Castellotti, Milan 1996.

A. Mariuz, "Giandomenico Tiepolo (1727–1804)," in *Giandomenico Tiepolo. Maestria e gioco. Disegni dal mondo*, exhibition catalogue (Castello, Udine, September 14–December 31, 1996; Indiana University Art Museum, Bloomington, January 15–March 9, 1997), edited by A.M. Gealt, G. Knox, Milan 1996, pp. 17–38.

1996–1999

La pittura nel Veneto. Il Cinquecento, edited by M. Lucco, 3 vols., Milan 1996–1999.

1997

E.M. Dal Pozzolo, "Tra Cariani e Rocco Marconi," in *Venezia Cinquecento*, VII, 13, 1997, pp. 5–37.

A. De Marchi, "Ritorno a Nicolò di Pietro," in *Nuovi Studi. Rivista di arte antica e moderna*, II, 3, 1997, pp. 5–24.

L. Sartor, "Lazzaro Bastiani e i suoi committenti," in *Arte Veneta*, 50, 1997, pp. 38–52.

"Il soffitto degli Scalzi di Giambattista Tiepolo," in *Quaderni della Soprintendenza per i Beni Artistici e Storici di Venezia*, 21, 1997.

A. Tempestini, *Giovanni Bellini*, Milan 1997.

1998

Antonio Pellegrini: il maestro veneto del Rococò alle corti d'Europa, exhibition catalogue (Palazzo della Ragione, Padua, September 20, 1998–January 10, 1999), edited by A. Bettagno, Venice 1998.

T. Franco, *Michele Giambono e il monumento a Cortesia da Serego in Santa Anastasia a Verona*, Padua 1998.

Lorenzo Lotto. Il genio inquieto del Rinascimento, exhibition catalogue (National Gallery of Art, Washington, November 2, 1997–March 1, 1998; Bergamo, Accademia Carrara di Belle Arti, April 2–June 28, 1998; Galeries Nationales du Grand Palais, Paris, October 13, 1998–January 11, 1999), edited by D.A. Brown, P. Humfrey, M. Lucco, Milan 1998.

F. Mazzocca, *Hayez*, Florence 1998.

1999

P. Benassai, *Sebastiano Mazzoni*, Florence 1999.

Da Leonardo a Canaletto. Disegni delle Gallerie dell'Accademia, exhibition catalogue (Gallerie dell'Accademia, Venice, April 24–July 25, 1999), edited by G. Nepi Scirè, A. Perissa Torrini, Milan 1999.

P. Hills, *Colore veneziano. Pittura, marmo, mosaico e vetro dal 1200 al 1550*, Milan 1999.

R. Klessmann, *Johann Liss*.

A Monograph and Catalogue Raisonné, Davaco 1999.
Il Rinascimento a Venezia e la pittura del Nord ai tempi di Bellini, Dürer e Tiziano, exhibition catalogue (Palazzo Grassi, Venice, September 5, 1999–January 9, 2000), edited by B. Aikema, B.L. Brown, Milan 1999.
M.G. Sarti, "'Muta predicatio': il 'San Giovanni Battista' di Tiziano," in *Venezia Cinquecento*, 17, IX, 1999, pp. 5–35.

2000
Antonio Canova e il suo ambiente artistico fra Venezia, Roma e Parigi, edited by G. Pavanello, Venice 2000.
I. Cecchini, *Quadri e commercio a Venezia durante il Seicento. Uno studio sul mercato dell'arte*, Venice 2000.
Il colore ritrovato. Bellini a Venezia, exhibition catalogue (Gallerie dell'Accademia, Venice, September 30, 2000–January 28, 2001), edited by R. Goffen, G. Nepi Scirè, Milan 2000.
P. Cottrell, "Corporate Colors: Bonifacio and Tintoretto at the Palazzo dei Camerlenghi in Venice," in *The Art Bulletin*, LXXXII, 4, December 2000, pp. 658–78.

2000–2001
La pittura nel Veneto. Il Seicento, edited by M. Lucco, 2 vols., Milan 2000–2001.

2001
Bergamo. L'altra Venezia. Il Rinascimento negli anni di Lorenzo Lotto 1510–1530, exhibition catalogue (Accademia Carrara, Bergamo, April 4–July 8, 2001), edited by F. Rossi, Cinisello Balsamo 2001.
M. Zanchi, *Andrea Previtali. Il coloritore prospettico di maniera belliniana*, Bergamo 2001.

2002
L. Caburlotto, "Un'equivoca fortuna: i primitivi nelle collezioni Correr e Molin," in *Arte Veneta*, 59, 2002, pp. 186–209.
Carlo Crivelli alle Gallerie dell'Accademia. Un capolavoro ricomposto, exhibition catalogue (Gallerie dell'Accademia, Venice,

November 29, 2002–February 2, 2003), Milan 2002.
Figure di collezionisti a Venezia tra Cinque e Seicento, edited by L. Borean, S. Mason, Udine 2002.
Il Trecento adriatico. Paolo Veneziano e la pittura tra Oriente e Occidente, exhibition catalogue (Castel Sismondo, Rimini, August 19–December 29, 2002), edited by F. Flores d'Arcais, G. Gentili, Cinisello Balsamo 2002.
Jacopo da Montagnana e la pittura padovana del secondo Quattrocento, proceedings from the study days (Montagnana and Padua, October 20–21, 1999), edited by A. De Nicolò Salmazo, G. Ericani, Padua 2002.
G. Scirè Nepi, A. Gentili, G. Romanelli, P. Rylands, *I dipinti di Venezia*, Udine 2002.

2002–2003
La pittura nel Veneto. L'Ottocento, edited by G. Pavanello, 2 vols., Milan 2002–2003.

2003
O. Ferrari, G. Scavizzi, *Luca Giordano. Nuove ricerche e inediti*, Naples 2003.
L. Finocchi Ghersi, *Il Rinascimento veneziano di Giovanni Bellini*, Venice 2003.
Fra' Galgario: le seduzioni del ritratto nel '700 europeo, exhibition catalogue (Accademia Carrara, Bergamo, October 2, 2003–January 11, 2004), edited by F. Rossi, Milan 2003.
Giorgione. "Le maraviglie dell'arte," exhibition catalogue (Gallerie dell'Accademia, Venice, November 1, 2003–February 22, 2004), edited by G. Nepi Scirè, S. Rossi, Venice 2003.
The Cambridge Companion to Titian, edited by P. Meilman, Cambridge 2003.
Capolavori che ritornano. Bellini e Vicenza, exhibition catalogue (Palazzo Thiene, Vicenza, December 5, 2003–January 25, 2004; Gallerie dell'Accademia, Venice, February 1–29, 2004), edited by F. Rigon, E.M. Dal

Pozzolo, Vicenza 2003.
Gaspare Traversi. Heiterkeit im Schatten, exhibition catalogue (Staatsgalerie, Stuttgart, 2003), edited by A.B. Rave, Stuttgart 2003.
A. Gentili, "Documenti e contesti per la committenza dell'ultimo Carpaccio," in *Venezia, le Marche e la civiltà adriatica: per festeggiare i 90 anni di Pietro Zampetti*, edited by I. Chiappini di Sorio, Monfalcone 2003, pp. 264–67.
G. Nepi Scirè, "La Sacra Famiglia con santa Caterina e san Giovanni Battista di Palma il Vecchio e Tiziano," in *Venezia, le Marche e la civiltà adriatica: per festeggiare i 90 anni di Pietro Zampetti*, edited by I. Chiappini di Sorio, Monfalcone 2003, pp. 294–97.
Titian, exhibition catalogue (National Gallery, London, February 19–May 18, 2003), edited by D. Jaffé, London 2003.

2004
F. Bottacin, *Tiberio Tinelli "Pittore e Cavaliere" (1587–1639)*, Mariano del Friuli 2004.
Natura e Maniera tra Tiziano e Caravaggio. Le ceneri violette di Giorgione, exhibition catalogue (Fruttiere di Palazzo Te, Mantua, September 5, 2004–January 9, 2005), edited by V. Sgarbi, M. Lucco, Milan 2004.
Carpaccio pittore di storie, exhibition catalogue (Gallerie dell'Accademia, Venice, November 27, 2004–March 13, 2005), edited by G. Nepi Scirè, Venice 2004.
Da Bellini a Veronese. Temi di arte veneta, edited by G. Toscano, F. Valcanover, Venice 2004.
E. Daffra, M. Ceriana, "Il polittico di San Bartolomeo di Cima da Conegliano," in *Arte Veneta*, 61, 2004, pp. 28–69.
A. De Nicolò Salmazo, *Andrea Mantegna*, Geneva–Milan 2004.
R. Lightbown, *Carlo Crivelli*, New Haven–London 2004.
Luce sul Settecento: Gaspare Traversi e l'arte del suo tempo in Emilia, exhibition catalogue (Galleria Nazionale, Parma,

April 4–July 4, 2004),
edited by L. Fornari Schianchi,
N. Spinosa, Naples 2004.
A. Mariuz, "Il paesaggio veneto
del Cinquecento," in *La pittura
di paesaggio in Italia. Il
Seicento*, edited by L. Trezzani,
Milan 2004, pp. 145–53.
*Ottocento veneto. Il trionfo
del colore*, exhibition catalogue
(Casa dei Carraresi, Treviso,
October 15, 2004–February 27,
2005), edited by G. Pavanello,
N. Stringa, Treviso 2004.
*Sebastiano Mazzoni. Storie
di Santa Caterina*, exhibition
catalogue (Gallerie
dell'Accademia, Venice, July
24–October 3, 2004), edited by
L. Caburlotto, Milan 2004.
*The Cambridge Companion
to Giovanni Bellini*, edited by
P. Humfrey, Cambridge 2004.
2005
"L'altro Veronese. Politica
e religione a Venezia negli anni
del disciplinamento,"
proceedings from the study days
(Università Ca' Foscari, Venice,
May 12–13, 2005),
edited by A. Gentili, in *Venezia
Cinquecento*, XV, 29,
January–June 2005.
"L'altro Veronese. Politica
e religione a Venezia negli
anni del disciplinamento,"
proceedings from the study days
(Università Ca' Foscari, Venice,
May 12–13, 2005), edited by A.
Gentili, in *Venezia Cinquecento*,
XV, 30, July–December 2005.
*Canaletto. Il trionfo della
veduta*, exhibition catalogue
(Palazzo Giustiniani, Rome,
March 12–June 19, 2005), edited
by A. Bettagno, B.A. Kowalczyk,
Cinisello Balsamo 2005.
*Il collezionismo a Venezia
e nel Veneto ai tempi della
Serenissima*, proceedings from
the conference (Palazzo Ducale,
Venice, September 21–25, 2003),
edited by B. Aikema, R. Lauber,
M. Seidel, Venice 2005.
A. Conti, *Storia del restauro e
della conservazione delle opere
d'arte*, Milan 2005.
F. Magani, "Veduta e capriccio:
sulle strade del Grand Tour," in
La pittura di paesaggio in

Italia. Il Settecento, edited by A.
Ottani Cavina, E. Calbi, Milan
2005, pp. 41–57.
*La natura morta alle Gallerie
dell'Accademia*, exhibition
catalogue (Gallerie
dell'Accademia, Venice,
September 6, 2005–January 8,
2006), edited by G. Nepi Scirè,
S. Rossi, Venice 2005.
*La pittura di paesaggio in
Italia. Il Settecento*, edited by A.
Ottani Cavina, E. Calbi, Milan
2005.
Ritratti e autoritratti d'artista,
exhibition catalogue (Gallerie
dell'Accademia, Venice, May
16–July 31, 2005), edited by
G. Nepi Scirè, Milan 2005.
*Tintoretto. Il ciclo di Santa
Caterina e la quadreria del
Palazzo Patriarcale*, exhibition
catalogue (Museo Diocesano,
Venice, October 6, 2005–July
30, 2006), edited
by G. Caputo, Milan 2005.
2006
Annibale Carracci, exhibition
catalogue (Museo Civico
Archeologico, Bologna,
September 22, 2006–January 7,
2007; DART, Chiostro del
Bramante, Rome, January
25–May 6, 2007), edited by D.
Benati, E. Riccomini, Milan
2006.
*Antonello da Messina. L'opera
completa*, exhibition catalogue
(Scuderie del Quirinale, Rome,
March 18–June 25, 2006),
edited by M. Lucco,
Milan 2006.
A. Ballarin, *La "Salomè"
del Romanino ed altri studi
sulla pittura bresciana del
Cinquecento*, edited by B.M.
Savy, Cittadella 2006.
*Bellini, Giorgione, Titian and
the Renaissance of the Venetian
Painting*, exhibition catalogue
(National Gallery of Art,
Washington, June 18–September
17, 2006; Vienna,
Kunsthistorisches Museum,
October 17, 2006–January 7,
2007), edited by D.A. Brown, S.
Ferino-Pagden, Milan 2006.
C. Guarnieri, *Lorenzo Veneziano*,
Cinisello Balsamo 2006.
R. Krischel, *Jacopo Tintoretto*.

Il miracolo dello schiavo,
Modena 2006.
Mantegna e Padova 1445–1460,
exhibition catalogue (Musei
Civici agli Eremitani, Padua,
September 16, 2006–January 14,
2007), edited by D. Banzato,
A. De Nicolò Salmazo, A.M.
Spiazzi, Milan 2006.
Mantegna e le Arti a Verona,
exhibition catalogue (Palazzo
della Gran Guardia, Verona,
September 16, 2006–January 14,
2007), edited by S. Marinelli,
P. Marini, Venice 2006.
*Mantegna a Mantova
1460–1506*, exhibition catalogue
(Palazzo Te, Mantua, September
16, 2006–January 14, 2007),
edited by M. Lucco, Milan 2006.
*Restituzioni 2006. Tesori d'arte
restaurati*, exhibition catalogue
(Gallerie di Palazzo Leoni
Montanari, Vicenza, March
25–June 11, 2006), edited
by C. Bertelli, Vicenza 2006.
*Romanino: un pittore nel
Rinascimento italiano*,
exhibition catalogue (Castello
del Buonconsiglio, Trento,
July 29–October 29, 2006),
edited by L. Camerlengo, E. Chini,
F. Frangi, F. De Gramatica,
Cinisello Balsamo 2006.
A. Scarpa, *Sebastiano Ricci*,
Milan 2006.
2007
*Collezionismo d'arte a Venezia.
Il Seicento*, edited by L. Borean,
S. Mason, Venice 2007.
*Cosmè Tura e Francesco del
Cossa. L'arte a Ferrara nell'età
di Borso d'Este*, exhibition
catalogue (Palazzo dei Diamanti,
Palazzo Schifanoia, Ferrara,
September 23, 2007–January 6,
2008), edited by M. Natale,
Ferrara 2007.
Dürer e l'Italia, exhibition
catalogue (Scuderie del
Quirinale, Rome, March
10–June 10, 2007),
edited by K. Herrmann Fiore,
Milan 2007.
L. Finocchi Ghersi, *Paolo
Veronese decoratore*, Venice
2007.
Tintoretto, exhibition catalogue
(Museo del Prado, Madrid,
January 30–May 13, 2007),

edited by M. Falomir, Madrid 2007.

Piero della Francesca e le corti italiane, exhibition catalogue (Museo Statale d'Arte Medievale e Moderna, Arezzo, March 31–July 22, 2007), edited by C. Bertelli, A. Paolucci, Milan 2007.

Rosalba Carriera "prima pittrice de l'Europa," exhibition catalogue (Galleria di Palazzo Cini a San Vio, Venice, September 1–October 28, 2007), edited by G. Pavanello, Venice 2007.

B. Sani, *Rosalba Carriera 1673-1757. Maestra del pastello nell'Europa ancien régime*, Turin 2007.

F. Spadotto, *Francesco Zuccarelli*, Milan 2007.

Venezia e l'Islam 828-1797, exhibition catalogue (Palazzo Ducale, Venice, July 28–November 25, 2007), edited by S. Carboni, Venice 2007.

Vittore Carpaccio. Tre capolavori restaurati, exhibition catalogue (Gallerie dell'Accademia, Venice, January 27–March 4, 2007), edited by G. Nepi Scirè, S. Rossi, Venice 2007.

Canova e la Venere Vincitrice, exhibition catalogue (Galleria Borghese, Rome, October 18, 2007–February 3, 2008), edited by A. Coliva, F. Mazzocca, Rome 2007.

2008

"Bellini a Venezia. Sette opere indagate nel loro contesto," edited by G. Poldi, G.C.F. Villa, *I Quaderni di Open Care 2*, Cinisello Balsamo 2008.

Canaletto e Bellotto. L'arte della veduta, exhibition catalogue (Palazzo Bricherasio, Turin, March 14–June 15, 2008), edited by B.A. Kowalczyk, Milan 2008.

Giovanni Baronzio e la pittura a Rimini nel Trecento, exhibition catalogue (Palazzo Barberini, Rome, March 13–May 18, 2008), edited by D. Ferrara, Cinisello Balsamo 2008.

Giovanni Bellini, exhibition catalogue (Scuderie del Quirinale, Rome, September 30, 2008–January 11, 2009), edited by M. Lucco, G.C.F. Villa, Cinisello Balsamo 2008.

Restituzioni 2008. Tesori d'arte restaurati, exhibition catalogue (Gallerie di Palazzo Leoni Montanari, Vicenza, March 29–June 29, 2008), edited by C. Bertelli, Venice 2008.

Salvator Rosa tra mito e magia, exhibition catalogue (Museo Capodimonte, Naples, April 18–June 29, 2008), Naples 2008.

Sebastiano del Piombo 1485-1547, exhibition catalogue (Palazzo Venice, Rome, February 8–May 18, 2008; Gemäldegalerie, Berlin, June 28–September 28, 2008), Milan 2008.

L'ultimo Tiziano e la sensualità della pittura, exhibition catalogue (Gallerie dell'Accademia, Venice, January 26–April 20, 2008), edited by S. Ferino-Pagden, Venice 2008.

Photograph Credits
Courtesy Ministero
dei Beni e delle Attività Culturali
e del Turismo:
Gallerie dell'Accademia di Venezia –
Archivio fotografico del Polo museale
del Veneto (photo Dino Zanella)
Archivio del Museo Correr
Archivio Mondadori Electa, Milano
Cameraphoto Arte, Venice
Foto Böhm, Venice

as well as
Matteo De Fina
Claudio Franzini
Mario Polesel

We wish to thank
Archivio fotografico
del Polo museale del Veneto,
Marina Amuro
and Diana Ziliotto

Editorial Coordination
Cristina Garbagna

Editing
Gail Swerling

Graphic Design
Tassinari/Vetta

Graphic Coordination
Angelo Galiotto

Page Layout
Elisa Seghezzi

Picture Research
Daniela Simone

Technical Coordination
Lara Panigas

Quality Control
Giancarlo Berti

This volume was printed by Mondadori Electa S.p.A.,
at Elcograf S.p.A., via Mondadori 15, Verona, in 2017